Hardy to

Selections from twelve poets of the twentieth century

Edited by Eric Williams

Edward Arnold

© Eric Williams 1976

First published 1976
by Edward Arnold (Publishers) Ltd
25 Hill Street, London W1X 8LL

ISBN: 0 7131 0041 9

Set in 11/12 Photon Baskerville and printed in Great Britain by
The Camelot Press Ltd, Southampton

Preface

This anthology is intended for students preparing for external examinations. In making extensive selections from the work of twelve poets writing during this century, my aim has been both to provide an introduction to the range of each poet's work and to include poems that will lend themselves to detailed comparison in discussion. In *Topics For Discussion* I have indicated some points of comparison that have proved fruitful when discussing the poems with students in the classroom, together with suggestions that could be used as starting-points for group discussion or by individual students preparing for written assignments.

Acknowledgments

The Publisher's thanks are due to the following for permission to use copyright material:
Faber & Faber Ltd for W. H. Auden's 'Night Mail', 'No Change of Place', 'Ode', 'Embassy', 'O What is that Sound', 'Refugee Blues', 'Epitaph on a Tyrant', 'Surgical Ward', 'Musée des Beaux Arts', 'The Unknown Citizen', 'As I Walked out one Evening', 'Our Bias', 'If I could Tell You' and 'On this Island' (Seascape) from *Collected Shorter Poems 1927–57*; Louis Macneice's 'Autobiography', 'Soap Suds', 'Solstice', 'Snow', 'The Sunlight on the Garden', 'Les Sylphides', 'Order to View', 'Débâcle', 'Prayer before Birth', 'Cradle Song for Eleanor', 'After the Crash', 'Budgie', 'The Gardener' and 'The Wiper' from *Collected Poems of Louis Macneice*; Ted Hughes' 'The Thought Fox', 'Wind', 'Hawk Roosting', 'Bayonet Charge', 'Six Young Men', 'The Horses' from *The Hawk in the Rain*, 'November', 'Crow Hill', 'Thrushes', 'Esther's Tomcat', 'Pike', 'Snowdrop', 'Dick Straightup' and 'The Bull Moses' from *Lupercal*, 'Her Husband' from *Poetry in the Making* and 'Thistles' from *Wodwo*, and for Philip Larkin's 'Days', 'The Whitsun Weddings', 'Mr Bleaney', 'Afternoons' and 'An Arundel Tomb' from *The Whitsun Weddings*, 'To the Sea', 'The Building', 'Going, Going', 'The Trees' and 'The Explosion' from *High Windows*; The Marvell Press for Philip Larkin's poems 'Born Yesterday' and 'Skin' from *The Less Deceived*; John Murray for John Betjeman's 'Pot Pourri from a Surrey Garden', 'A Subaltern's Love Song', 'Indoor Games near Newbury', 'Winter Seascape', 'Greenway', 'East Anglian Bathe', 'Sunday Morning, King's Cambridge', 'Bristol and Clifton', 'The Village Inn', 'Inexpensive Progress', 'Death in Leamington', 'On a Portrait of a Deaf Man' and 'A Child Ill' from *Collected Poems*; Macmillan & Co. Ltd for Charles Causley's 'John Polruddon', 'Nelson Gardens', 'By St Thomas' Water', 'Dockacre', 'Reservoir Street' and 'Mary, Mary Magdalene' from *Collected Poems*; Cassell & Co. Ltd and A. P. Watt and Robert Graves for his poems 'On Rising Early', 'The Cool Web', 'Lost Love', 'Not at Home', 'The Haunted House', 'Surgical Ward: Men', 'The Pier Glass', 'The Face in the Mirror', 'A Slice of Wedding Cake', 'Counting the Beats' and 'The Welsh Incident' from *Collected Poems of 1965*, 'Recalling War' from *Collected Poems 1959*, 'The Alice Jean' from *The Penny Fiddle*, 'Conversation Piece'

and 'The Leveller' from *Collected Poems 1975*; Macmillan Publishers Ltd, London and Basingstoke, and The Trustees of the Hardy Estate for 'The Darkling Thrush', 'Afterwards', 'After a Journey', 'At Castle Boterel', 'A Thunderstorm in Town', 'A Night in November', 'The Self-Unseeing', 'An August Midnight', 'At Middle-Field Gate in February', 'Beyond the Last Lamp', 'Silences', 'Old Furniture', 'During Wind and Rain', 'In Time of the "Breaking of Nations"' and 'He Never Expected Much'; Laurence Pollinger Ltd and the Estate of the late Mrs Frieda Lawrence for D. H. Lawrence's poems 'Piano', 'The Collier's Wife', 'At the Window', 'Brooding Grief', 'Giorno Dei Morti', 'Bat', 'Snake', 'Kangaroo', 'Humming Bird', 'Bavarian Gentians', 'Work' and 'Money Madness' from *The Complete Poems of D. H. Lawrence*; André Deutsch Ltd for Laurie's Lee's 'Sunken Evening', 'Apples' and 'Town Owl' from *My Many Coated Man*; The Hogarth Press Ltd for Laurie's Lee's 'The Long War' from *The Sun my Monument* and Laurie Lee for his poems 'Cock Pheasant', 'Thistle', 'April Rise', 'Day of these Days', 'First Love', 'Milkmaid', 'Field of Autumn' and 'Christmas Candles'; The Wilfred Owen Estate and Chatto and Windus Ltd for Wilfred Owen's poems 'Exposure', 'Dulce et Decorum Est', 'Futility', 'Anthem for Doomed Youth', 'The Sentry', 'Apologia', 'Pro Poemate Meo', 'Insensibility', 'The Send-Off' and 'Strange Meeting' from *The Collected Poems of Wilfred Owen*, ed. C. Day Lewis; Rupert Hart-Davis Ltd for Charles Causley's poems 'The Seasons in North Cornwall', 'Nursery Rhyme of Innocence and Experience', 'Cowboy Song', 'Song of the Dying Gunner A.A.1', 'Convoy' and 'Death of an Aircraft' from *Union Street*, 'Charlotte Dymond', 'Innocent Song' and 'Death of a Poet' from *Johnny Alleluia*; Granada Publishing Ltd and Rupert Hart-Davis Ltd for R. S. Thomas' poems 'Song', 'Soil', 'Welsh Landscape', 'Depopulation of the Hills', 'The Village', 'Affinity', 'The Lonely Farmer', 'A Peasant', 'Invasion on the Farm', 'Cynddylan on a Tractor', 'Death of a Peasant' and 'The Evacuee' from *Song at the Year's Turning*.

Contents

Thomas Hardy

The Darkling Thrush

I leant upon a coppice gate
    When Frost was spectre-gray,
And Winter's dregs made desolate
    The weakening eye of day.
The tangled bine-stems scored the sky
    Like strings of broken lyres,
And all mankind that haunted nigh
    Had sought their household fires.

The land's sharp features seemed to be
    The Century's corpse outleant,
His crypt the cloudy canopy,
    The wind his death-lament.
The ancient pulse of germ and birth
    Was shrunken hard and dry,
And every spirit upon earth
    Seemed fervourless as I.

At once a voice arose among
    The bleak twigs overhead
In a full-hearted evensong
    Of joy illimited;
An aged thrush, frail, gaunt, and small,
    In blast-beruffled plume,
Had chosen thus to fling his soul
    Upon the growing gloom.

So little cause for carolings
    Of such ecstatic sound
Was written on terrestrial things
    Afar or nigh around,
That I could think there trembled through
    His happy good-night air
Some blessed Hope, whereof he knew
    And I was unaware.

Afterwards

When the Present has latched its postern behind my tremulous
stay,
  And the May month flaps its glad green leaves like wings,
Delicate-filmed as new-spun silk, will the neighbours say,
  'He was a man who used to notice such things'?

If it be in the dusk when, like an eyelid's soundless blink,
  The dewfall-hawk comes crossing the shades to alight
Upon the wind-warped upland thorn, a gazer may think,
  'To him this must have been a familiar sight.'

If I pass during some nocturnal blackness, mothy and warm,
  When the hedgehog travels furtively over the lawn,
One may say, 'He strove that such innocent creatures should come
to no harm,
  But he could do little for them; and now he is gone.'

If, when hearing that I have been stilled at last, they stand at the
door,
  Watching the full-starred heavens that winter sees,
Will this thought rise on those who will meet my face no more,
  'He was one who had an eye for such mysteries'?

And will any say when my bell of quittance is heard in the gloom,
  And a crossing breeze cuts a pause in its outrollings,
Till they rise again, as they were a new bell's boom,
  'He hears it not now, but used to notice such things'?

An August Midnight

A shaded lamp and a waving blind,
And the beat of a clock from a distant floor:
On this scene enter—winged, horned, and spined—
A longlegs, a moth, and a dumbledore;
While 'mid my page there idly stands
A sleepy fly, that rubs its hands . . .

Thus meet we five, in this still place,
At this point of time, at this point in space,
—My guests besmear my new-penned line,
Or bang at the lamp and fall supine.
'God's humblest, they!' I muse. Yet why?
They know Earth-secrets that know not I.

At Middle-field Gate In February

The bars are thick with drops that show
    As they gather themselves from the fog
Like silver buttons ranged in a row,
And as evenly spaced as if measured, although
    They fall at the feeblest jog.

They load the leafless hedge hard by,
    And the blades of last year's grass,
While the fallow ploughland turned up nigh
In raw rolls, clammy and clogging lie—
    Too clogging for feet to pass.

How dry it was on a far-back day
    When straws hung the hedge and around,
When amid the sheaves in amorous play
In curtained bonnets and light array
    Bloomed a bevy now underground!

The Self-Unseeing

Here is the ancient floor,
Footworn and hollowed and thin,
Here was the former door
Where the dead feet walked in.

She sat here in her chair,
Smiling into the fire;
He who played stood there,
Bowing it higher and higher.

Childlike, I danced in a dream;
Blessings emblazoned that day;
Everything glowed with a gleam;
Yet we were looking away!

A Night In November

I marked when the weather changed,
And the panes began to quake,
And the winds rose up and ranged,
That night, lying half-awake.

Dead leaves blew into my room,
And alighted upon my bed,
And a tree declared to the gloom
Its sorrow that they were shed.

One leaf of them touched my hand,
And I thought that it was you
There stood as you used to stand,
And saying at last you knew!

A Thunderstorm In Town

She wore a new 'terra-cotta' dress,
And we stayed, because of the pelting storm,
Within the hansom's dry recess,
Though the horse had stopped; yea, motionless
    We sat on, snug and warm.

Then the downpour ceased, to my sharp sad pain
And the glass that had screened our forms before
Flew up, and out she sprang to her door:
I should have kissed her if the rain
    Had lasted a minute more.

Beyond The Last Lamp
(near Tooting Common)

While rain, with eve in partnership,
Descended darkly, drip, drip, drip,
Beyond the last lone lamp I passed
 Walking slowly, whispering sadly,
 Two linked loiterers, wan, downcast:
Some heavy thought constrained each face,
And blinded them to time and place.

The pair seemed lovers, yet absorbed
In mental scenes no longer orbed
By love's young rays. Each countenance
 As it slowly, as it sadly
 Caught the lamplight's yellow glance,
Held in suspense a misery
At things which had been or might be.

When I retrod that watery way
Some hours beyond the droop of day,
Still I found pacing there the twain
 Just as slowly, just as sadly,
 Heedless of the night and rain.
One could but wonder who they were
And what wild woe detained them there.

Though thirty years of blur and blot
Have slid since I beheld that spot,
And saw in curious converse there
 Moving slowly, moving sadly
 That mysterious tragic pair,
Its olden look may linger on—
All but the couple, they have gone.

Whither? Who knows, indeed. . . . And yet
To me, when nights are weird and wet,
Without those comrades there at tryst
 Creeping slowly, creeping sadly,
 That lone lane does not exist.
There they seem brooding on their pain,
And will, while such a lane remain.

The Voice

Woman much missed, how you call to me, call to me,
Saying that now you are not as you were
When you had changed from the one who was all to me,
But as at first, when our day was fair.

Can it be you that I hear? Let me view you, then,
Standing as when I drew near to the town
Where you would wait for me: yes, as I knew you then,
Even to the original air-blue gown!

Or is it only the breeze, in its listlessness
Travelling across the wet mead to me here,
You being ever dissolved to wan wistlessness,
Heard no more again far or near?

    Thus I; faltering forward,
    Leaves around me falling,
Wind oozing thin through the thorn from norward,
    And the woman calling.

After A Journey

Hereto I come to view a voiceless ghost;
    Whither, O whither will its whim now draw me?
Up the cliff, down, till I'm lonely, lost,
    And the unseen waters' ejaculations awe me.
Where you will next be there's no knowing,
    Facing round about me everywhere,
      With your nut-coloured hair,
And gray eyes, and rose-flush coming and going.

Yes: I have re-entered your olden haunts at last;
    Through the years, through the dead scenes I have tracked you;
What have you now found to say of our past—
    Scanned across the dark space wherein I have lacked you?
Summer gave us sweets, but autumn wrought division?
    Things were not lastly as firstly well
      With us twain, you tell?
But all's closed now, despite Time's derision.

I see what you are doing: you are leading me on
    To the spots we knew when we haunted here together,
The waterfall, above which the mist-bow shone
    At the then fair hour in the then fair weather,
And the cave just under, with a voice still so hollow
    That it seems to call out to me from forty years ago,
        When you were all aglow,
And not the thin ghost that I now frailly follow!

Ignorant of what there is flitting here to see,
    The waked birds preen and the seals flop lazily;
Soon you will have, Dear, to vanish from me,
    For the stars close their shutters and the dawn whitens hazily.
Trust me, I mind not, though Life lours,
    The bringing me here; nay, bring me here again!
        I am just the same as when
Our days were a joy, and our paths through flowers.

At Castle Boterel

As I drive to the junction of lane and highway,
    And the drizzle bedrenches the waggonette,
I look behind at the fading byway,
    And see on its slope, now glistening wet,
        Distinctly yet

Myself and a girlish form benighted
    In dry March weather. We climb the road
Beside a chaise. We had just alighted
    To ease the sturdy pony's load
        When he sighed and slowed.

What we did as we climbed, and what we talked of
    Matters not much, nor to what it led,—
Something that life will not be balked of
    Without rude reason till hope is dead,
        And feeling fled.

It filled but a minute. But was there ever
    A time of such quality, since or before,
In that hill's story? To one mind never,
    Though it has been climbed, foot-swift, foot-sore,
        By thousands more.

Primaeval rocks form the road's steep border,
  And much have they faced there, first and last,
Of the transitory in Earth's long order;
  But what they record in colour and cast
    Is—that we two passed.

And to me, though Time's unflinching rigour,
  In mindless rote, has ruled from sight
The substance now, one phantom figure
  Remains on the slope, as when that night
    Saw us alight.

I look and see it there, shrinking, shrinking,
  I look back at it amid the rain
For the very last time; for my sand is sinking,
  And I shall traverse old love's domain
    Never again.

Silences

There is the silence of a copse or croft
  When the wind sinks dumb,
    And of a belfry-loft
When the tenor after tolling stops its hum.

And there's the silence of a lonely pond
  Where a man was drowned,
    Nor nigh nor yond
A newt, frog, toad, to make the merest sound.

But the rapt silence of an empty house
  Where oneself was born,
    Dwelt, held carouse
With friends, is of all silences most forlorn!

Past are remembered songs and music-strains
  Once audible there:
    Roof, rafters, panes
Look absent-thoughted, tranced, or locked in prayer.

It seems no power on earth can waken it
Or rouse its rooms,
Or its past permit
The present to stir a torpor like a tomb's.

Old Furniture

I know not how it may be with others
Who sit amid relics of householdry
That date from the days of their mothers' mothers,
But well I know how it is with me
Continually.

I see the hands of the generations
That owned each shiny familiar thing
In play on its knobs and indentations,
And with its ancient fashioning
Still dallying:

Hands behind hands, growing paler and paler,
As in a mirror a candle-flame
Shows images of itself, each frailer
As it recedes, though the eye may frame
Its shape the same.

On the clock's dull dial a foggy finger,
Moving to set the minutes right
With tentative touches that lift and linger
In the wont of a moth on a summer night,
Creeps to my sight.

On this old viol, too, fingers are dancing—
As whilom— just over the strings by the nut,
The tip of a bow receding, advancing
In airy quivers, as if it would cut
The plaintive gut.

And I see a face by that box for tinder,
Glowing forth in fits from the dark,
And fading again, as the linten cinder
Kindles to red at the flinty spark,
Or goes out stark.

Well, well. It is best to be up and doing,
  The world has no use for one to-day
Who eyes things thus—no aim pursuing!
  He should not continue in this stay,
    But sink away.

During Wind And Rain

  They sing their dearest songs—
  He, she, all of them—yea,
  Treble and tenor and bass,
    And one to play;
  With the candles mooning each face. . . .
    Ah, no; the years O!
How the sick leaves reel down in throngs!

  They clear the creeping moss—
  Elders and juniors—aye,
  Making the pathways neat
    And the garden gay;
  And they build a shady seat. . . .
    Ah, no; the years, the years;
See, the white storm-birds wing across!

  They are blithely breakfasting all—
  Men and maidens—yea,
  Under the summer tree,
    With a glimpse of the bay,
  While pet fowl come to the knee. . . .
    Ah, no; the years O!
And the rotten rose is ript from the wall.

  They change to a high new house,
  He, she, all of them—aye,
  Clocks and carpets and chairs
    On the lawn all day,
  And brightest things that are theirs. . . .
    Ah, no; the years, the years;
Down their carved names the rain-drop ploughs.

In Time Of 'The Breaking Of Nations'

1

Only a man harrowing clods
   In a slow silent walk
With an old horse that stumbles and nods
   Half asleep as they stalk.

2

Only thin smoke without flame
   From the heaps of couch-grass;
Yet this will go onward the same
   Though Dynasties pass.

3

Yonder a maid and her wight
   Come whispering by:
War's annals will cloud into night
   Ere their story die.

He Never Expected Much
(or)
A Consideration On My Eighty-Sixth Birthday

Well, World, you have kept faith with me,
   Kept faith with me;
Upon the whole you have proved to be
   Much as you said you were.
Since as a child I used to lie
Upon the leaze and watch the sky,
Never, I own, expected I
   That life would all be fair.

'Twas then you said, and since have said,
   Times since have said,
In that mysterious voice you shed
   From clouds and hills around:
'Many have loved me desperately,
Many with smooth serenity,
While some have shown contempt of me
   Till they dropped underground.

'I do not promise overmuch,
    Child; overmuch;
Just neutral-tinted haps and such,'
    You said to minds like mine.
Wise warning for your credit's sake!
Which I for one failed not to take,
And hence could stem such strain and ache
    As each year might assign.

Wilfred Owen

Exposure

Our brains ache, in the merciless iced east winds that knive us . . .
Wearied we keep awake because the night is silent . . .
Low, drooping flares confuse our memory of the salient . . .
Worried by silence, sentries whisper, curious, nervous,
    But nothing happens.

Watching, we hear the mad gusts tugging on the wire,
Like twitching agonies of men among its brambles.
Northward, incessantly, the flickering gunnery rumbles,
Far off, like a dull rumour of some other war.
    What are we doing here?

The poignant misery of dawn begins to grow . . .
We only know war lasts, rain soaks, and clouds sag stormy.
Dawn massing in the east her melancholy army
Attacks once more in ranks on shivering ranks of gray,
    But nothing happens.

Sudden successive flights of bullets streak the silence.
Less deadly than the air that shudders black with snow,
With sidelong flowing flakes that flock, pause, and renew,
We watch them wandering up and down the wind's nonchalance,
    But nothing happens.

Pale flakes with fingering stealth come feeling for our faces—
We cringe in holes, back on forgotten dreams, and stare, snow-
                        dazed,
Deep into grassier ditches. So we drowse, sun-dozed,
Littered with blossoms trickling where the blackbird fusses.
    Is it that we are dying?

Slowly our ghosts drag home: glimpsing the sunk fires, glozed
With crusted dark-red jewels; crickets jingle there;
For hours the innocent mice rejoice: the house is theirs;
Shutters and doors, all closed: on us the doors are closed,—
     We turn back to our dying.

Since we believe not otherwise can kind fires burn;
Nor ever suns smile true on child, or field, or fruit.
For God's invincible spring our love is made afraid;
Therefore, not loath, we lie out here; therefore were born,
     For love of God seems dying.

To-night, His frost will fasten on this mud and us,
Shrivelling many hands, puckering foreheads crisp.
The burying-party, picks and shovels in their shaking grasp,
Pause over half-known faces. All their eyes are ice,
     But nothing happens.

Dulce Et Decorum Est

Bent double, like old beggars under sacks,
Knock-kneed, coughing like hags, we cursed through sludge,
Till on the haunting flares we turned our backs,
And towards our distant rest began to trudge.
Men marched asleep. Many had lost their boots,
But limped on, blood-shod. All went lame, all blind;
Drunk with fatigue; deaf even to the hoots
Of gas-shells dropping softly behind.

Gas! GAS! Quick, boys!—An ecstasy of fumbling,
Fitting the clumsy helmets just in time,
But someone still was yelling out and stumbling
And floundering like a man in fire or lime.—
Dim through the misty panes and thick green light,
As under a green sea, I saw him drowning.

In all my dreams before my helpless sight
He plunges at me, guttering, choking, drowning.

If in some smothering dreams, you too could pace
Behind the wagon that we flung him in,
And watch the white eyes writhing in his face,
His hanging face, like a devil's sick of sin;
If you could hear, at every jolt, the blood
Come gargling from the froth-corrupted lungs,
Bitter as the cud
Of vile, incurable sores on innocent tongues,—
My friend, you would not tell with such high zest
To children ardent for some desperate glory,
The old Lie: Dulce et decorum est
Pro patria mori.

Futility

Move him into the sun—
Gently its touch awoke him once,
At home, whispering of fields unsown.
Always it woke him, even in France,
Until this morning and this snow.
If anything might rouse him now
The kind old sun will know.

Think how it wakes the seeds,—
Woke, once, the clays of a cold star.
Are limbs, so dear-achieved, are sides,
Full-nerved—still warm—too hard to stir?
Was it for this the clay grew tall?
—O what made fatuous sunbeams toil
To break earth's sleep at all?

Anthem For Doomed Youth

What passing-bells for these who die as cattle?
    Only the monstrous anger of the guns.
    Only the stuttering rifles' rapid rattle
Can patter out their hasty orisons.
No mockeries for them from prayers or bells,
    Nor any voice of mourning save the choirs,—
The shrill, demented choirs of wailing shells;
    And bugles calling for them from sad shires.

What candles may be held to speed them all?
   Not in the hands of boys, but in their eyes
Shall shine the holy glimmers of good-byes.
   The pallor of girls' brows shall be their pall;
Their flowers the tenderness of silent minds,
And each slow dusk a drawing-down of blinds.

The Sentry

We'd found an old Boche dug-out, and he knew,
And gave us hell, for shell on frantic shell
Hammered on top, but never quite burst through.
Rain, guttering down in waterfalls of slime
Kept slush waist-high that, rising hour by hour,
Choked up the steps too thick with clay to climb.
What murk of air remained stank old, and sour
With fumes of whizz-bangs, and the smell of men
Who'd lived there years, and left their curse in the den,
If not their corpses. . . .
                    There we herded from the blast
Of whizz-bangs, but one found our door at last,—
Buffeting eyes and breath, snuffing the candles.
And thud! flump! thud! down the steep steps came thumping
And splashing in the flood, deluging muck—
The sentry's body; then, his rifle, handles
Of old Boche bombs, and mud in ruck on ruck.
We dredged him up, for killed, until he whined
'O sir, my eyes—I'm blind—I'm blind, I'm blind!'
Coaxing, I held a flame against his lids
And said if he could see the last blurred light
He was not blind; in time he'd get all right.
'I can't,' he sobbed. Eyeballs, huge-bulged like squids',
Watch my dreams still; but I forgot him there
In posting next for duty, and sending a scout
To beg a stretcher somewhere, and floundering about
To other posts under the shrieking air.

           .   .   .   .

Those other wretches, how they bled and spewed,
And one who would have drowned himself for good,—
I try not to remember these things now.
Let dread hark back for one word only: how
Half listening to that sentry's moans and jumps,
And the wild chattering of his broken teeth,
Renewed most horribly whenever crumps
Pummelled the roof and slogged the air beneath—
Through the dense din, I say, we heard him shout
'I see your lights!' But ours had long died out.

Apologia Pro Poemate Meo

I, too, saw God through mud—
    The mud that cracked on cheeks when wretches smiled.
    War brought more glory to their eyes than blood,
    And gave their laughs more glee than shakes a child.

Merry it was to laugh there—
    Where death becomes absurd and life absurder.
    For power was on us as we slashed bones bare
    Not to feel sickness or remorse of murder.

I, too have dropped off fear—
    Behind the barrage, dead as my platoon,
    And sailed my spirit surging, light and clear
    Past the entanglement where hopes lay strewn;

And witnessed exultation—
    Faces that used to curse me, scowl for scowl,
    Shine and lift up with passion of oblation,
    Seraphic for an hour; though they were foul.

I have made fellowships—
    Untold of happy lovers in old song.
    For love is not the binding of fair lips
    With the soft silk of eyes that look and long,

By Joy, whose ribbon slips,—
    But wound with war's hard wire whose stakes are strong;
    Bound with the bandage of the arm that drips;
    Knit in the webbing of the rifle-thong.

I have perceived much beauty
    In the hoarse oaths that kept our courage straight;
    Hear music in the silentness of duty;
    Found peace where shell-storms spouted reddest spate.

Nevertheless, except you share
    With them in hell the sorrowful dark of hell,
    Whose world is but the trembling of a flare,
    And heaven but as the highway for a shell,

You shall not hear their mirth:
    You shall not come to think them well content
    By any jest of mine. These men are worth
    Your tears. You are not worth their merriment.

Insensibility

I

Happy are men who yet before they are killed
Can let their veins run cold.
Whom no compassion fleers
Or makes their feet
Sore on the alleys cobbled with their brothers.
The front line withers,
But they are troops who fade, not flowers,
For poets' tearful fooling:
Men, gaps for filling:
Losses who might have fought
Longer, but no one bothers.

II

And some cease feeling
Even themselves or for themselves.
Dullness best solves
The tease and doubt of shelling,
And Chance's strange arithmetic
Comes simpler than the reckoning of their shilling.
They keep no check on armies' decimation.

III

Happy are these who lose imagination:
They have enough to carry with ammunition.
Their spirit drags no pack,
Their old wounds save with cold can not more ache.
Having seen all things red,
Their eyes are rid
Of the hurt of the colour of blood for ever.
And terror's first constriction over,
Their hearts remain small-drawn.
Their senses in some scorching cautery of battle
Now long since ironed,
Can laugh among the dying, unconcerned.

IV

Happy the soldier home, with not a notion
How somewhere, every dawn, some men attack,
And many sighs are drained.
Happy the lad whose mind was never trained:
His days are worth forgetting more than not.
He sings along the march
Which we march taciturn, because of dusk,
The long, forlorn, relentless trend
From larger day to huger night.

V

We wise, who with a thought besmirch
Blood over all our soul,
How should we see our task
But through his blunt and lashless eyes?
Alive, he is not vital overmuch;
Dying, not mortal overmuch;
Nor sad, nor proud,
Nor curious at all.
He cannot tell
Old men's placidity from his.

VI

But cursed are dullards whom no cannon shuns,
That they should be as stones;
Wretched are they, and mean
With paucity that never was simplicity.
By choice they made themselves immune
To pity and whatever moans in man
Before the last sea and the hapless stars;
Whatever mourns when many leave these shores,
Whatever shares
The eternal reciprocity of tears.

The Send-Off

Down the close, darkening lanes they sang their way
To the siding-shed,
And lined the train with faces grimly gay.

Their breasts were stuck all white with wreath and spray
As men's are, dead.

Dull porters watched them, and a casual tramp
Stood staring hard,
Sorry to miss them from the upland camp.
Then, unmoved, signals nodded, and a lamp
Winked to the guard

So secretly, like wrongs hushed up, they went.
They were not ours:
We never heard to which front these were sent.

Nor there if they yet mock what women meant
Who gave them flowers.

Shall they return to beatings of great bells
In wild train-loads?
A few, too few for drums and yells,
May creep back, silent, to village wells
Up half-known roads.

Strange Meeting

It seemed that out of battle I escaped
Down some profound dull tunnel, long since scooped
Through granites which titanic wars had groined.
Yet also there encumbered sleepers groaned,
Too fast in thought or death to be bestirred.
Then, as I probed them, one sprang up, and stared
With piteous recognition in fixed eyes,
Lifting distressful hands as if to bless.
And by his smile, I knew that sullen hall,
By his dead smile I knew we stood in Hell.
With a thousand pains that vision's face was grained;
Yet no blood reached there from the upper ground,
And no guns thumped, or down the flues made moan.
'Strange friend,' I said, 'here is no cause to mourn.'
'None,' said the other,' save the undone years,
The hopelessness. Whatever hope is yours,
Was my life also; I went hunting wild
After the wildest beauty in the world,
Which lies not calm in eyes, or braided hair,
But mocks the steady running of the hour,
And if it grieves, grieves richlier than here.
For by my glee might many men have laughed,
And of my weeping something had been left,
Which must die now. I mean the truth untold,
The pity of war, the pity war distilled.
Now men will go content with what we spoiled.
Or, discontent, boil bloody, and be spilled.
They will be swift with swiftness of the tigress,
None will break ranks, though nations trek from progress.
Courage was mine, and I had mystery,
Wisdom was mine, and I had mastery;
To miss the march of this retreating world
Into vain citadels that are not walled.
Then, when much blood had clogged their chariot-wheels
I would go up and wash them from sweet wells,
Even with truths that lie too deep for taint.
I would have poured my spirit without stint
But not through wounds; not on the cess of war.
Foreheads of men have bled where no wounds were.

I am the enemy you killed, my friend.
I knew you in this dark; for so you frowned
Yesterday through me as you jabbed and killed.
I parried; but my hands were loath and cold.
Let us sleep now. . . .'

Robert Graves

On Rising Early

Rising early and walking in the garden
Before the sun has properly climbed the hill—
His rays warming the roof, not yet the grass
That is white with dew still.

And not enough breeze to eddy a puff of smoke,
And out in the meadows a thick mist lying yet,
And nothing anywhere ill or noticeable—
Thanks indeed for that.

But was there ever a day with wit enough
To be always early, to draw the smoke up straight
Even at three o'clock of an afternoon,
To spare dullness or sweat?

Indeed, many such days I remember
That were dew-white and gracious to the last,
That ruled out meal-times, yet had no more hunger
Than was felt by rising a half-hour before breakfast,
Nor more fatigue—where was it that I went
So unencumbered, with my feet trampling
Like strangers on the past?

The Cool Web

Children are dumb to say how hot the day is,
How hot the scent is of the summer rose,
How dreadful the black wastes of evening sky,
How dreadful the tall soldiers drumming by.

But we have speech, to chill the angry day,
And speech, to dull the rose's cruel scent.
We spell away the overhanging night,
We spell away the soldiers and the fright.

There's a cool web of language winds us in,
Retreat from too much joy or too much fear:
We grow sea-green at last and coldly die
In brininess and volubility.

But if we let our tongues lose self-possession,
Throwing off language and its watery clasp
Before our death, instead of when death comes,
Facing the wide glare of the children's day,
Facing the rose, the dark sky and the drums,
We shall go mad no doubt and die that way.

Lost Love

His eyes are quickened so with grief,
He can watch a grass or leaf
Every instant grow; he can
Clearly through a flint wall see,
Or watch the startled spirit flee
From the throat of a dead man.
   Across two counties he can hear
And catch your words before you speak.
The woodlouse or the maggot's weak
Clamour rings in his sad ear,
And noise so slight it would surpass
Credence—drinking sound of grass,
Worm talk, clashing jaws of moth
Chumbling holes in cloth;
The groan of ants who undertake
Gigantic loads for honour's sake
(Their sinews creak, their breath comes thin);
Whir of spiders when they spin,
And minute whispering, mumbling, sighs
Of idle grubs and flies.
   This man is quickened so with grief,
He wanders god-like or like thief
Inside and out, below, above,
Without relief seeking lost love.

Not At Home

Her house loomed at the end of a Berkshire lane,
Tall but retired. She was expecting me;
And I approached with light heart and quick tread,
Having already seen from the garden gate
How bright her knocker shone—in readiness
For my confident rap?—and the steps holystoned.
I ran the last few paces, rapped and listened
Intently for the rustle of her approach. . . .

No reply, no movement. I waited three long minutes,
Then, in surprise, went down the path again
To observe the chimney stacks. No smoke from either.
And the curtains: were they drawn against the sun?
Or against what, then? I glanced over a wall
At her well-tended orchard, heavy with bloom
(Easter fell late that year, Spring had come early),
And found the gardener, bent over cold frames.

'Her ladyship is not at home?'
                              'No, sir.'
'She was expecting me. My name is Lion.
Did she leave a note?'
                    'No, sir, she left no note.'
'I trust nothing has happened . . .?'
                              'No, sir, nothing . . .
And yet she seemed preoccupied: we guess
Some family reason.'
                    '*Has* she a family?'
'That, sir, I could not say. . . . She seemed distressed—
Not quite herself, if I may venture so.'
'But she left no note?'
                    'Only a verbal message:
Her ladyship will be away some weeks
Or months, hopes to return before midsummer,
And, please, you are not to communicate.
There was something else: about the need for patience.'

The sun went in, a bleak wind shook the blossom,
Dust flew, the windows glared in a blank row. . . .
And yet I felt, when I turned slowly away,
Her eyes boring my back, as it might be posted
Behind a curtain slit, and still in love.

Welsh Incident

'But that was nothing to what things came out
From the sea-caves of Criccieth yonder.'
'What were they? Mermaids? dragons? ghosts?'
'Nothing at all of any things like that.'
'What were they, then?'
                              'All sorts of queer things,
Things never seen or heard or written about,
Very strange, un-Welsh, utterly peculiar
Things. Oh, solid enough they seemed to touch,
Had anyone dared it. Marvellous creation,
All various shapes and sizes, and no sizes,
All new, each perfectly unlike his neighbour,
Though all came moving slowly out together.'
'Describe just one of them.'
                              'I am unable.'
'What were their colours?'
                              'Mostly nameless colours,
Colours you'd like to see; but one was puce
Or perhaps more like crimson, but not purplish.
Some had no colour.'
                     'Tell me, had they legs?'
'Not a leg nor foot among them that I saw.'
'But did these things come out in any order?
What o'clock was it? What was the day of the week?
Who else was present? How was the weather?'
'I was coming to that. It was half-past three
On Easter Tuesday last. The sun was shining.
The Harlech Silver Band played *Marchog Jesu*
On thirty-seven shimmering instruments,
Collecting for Caernarvon's (Fever) Hospital Fund.
The populations of Pwllheli, Criccieth,
Portmadoc, Borth, Tremadoc, Penrhyndeudraeth,
Were all assembled. Criccieth's mayor addressed them
First in good Welsh and then in fluent English,
Twisting his fingers in his chain of office,
Welcoming the things. They came out on the sand,
Not keeping time to the band, moving seaward
Silently at a snail's pace. But at last
The most odd, indescribable thing of all,
Which hardly one man there could see for wonder,
Did something recognizably a something.'

'Well, what?'
        'It made a noise.'
                'A frightening noise?'
'No, no.'
        'A musical noise? A noise of scuffling?'
'No, but a very loud, respectable noise—
Like groaning to oneself on Sunday morning
In Chapel, close before the second psalm.'
'What did the mayor do?'
                'I was coming to that.'

The *Alice Jean*

One moonlight night a ship drove in,
  A ghost ship from the west,
Drifting with bare mast and lone tiller;
  Like a mermaid drest
In long green weed and barnacles
  She beached and came to rest.

All the watchers of the coast
  Flocked to view the sight;
Men and women, streaming down
  Through the summer night,
Found her standing tall and ragged
  Beached in the moonlight.

Then one old woman stared aghast:
  'The *Alice Jean*? But no!
The ship that took my Ned from me
  Sixty years ago—
Drifted back from the utmost west
  With the ocean's flow?

'Caught and caged in the weedy pool
  Beyond the western brink,
Where crewless vessels lie and rot
  In waters black as ink.
Torn out at last by a sudden gale—
  Is it the *Jean*, you think?'

A hundred women gaped at her,
   The menfolk nudged and laughed,
But none could find a likelier story
   For the strange craft
With fear and death and desolation
   Rigged fore and aft.

The blind ship came forgotten home
   To all but one of these,
Of whom none dared to climb aboard her:
   And by and by the breeze
Veered hard about, and the *Alice Jean*
   Foundered in foaming seas.

The Haunted House

'Come, surly fellow, come: a song!'
   What, fools? Sing to you?
Choose from the clouded tales of wrong
   And terror I bring to you:

Of a night so torn with cries,
   Honest men sleeping
Start awake with rabid eyes,
   Bone-chilled, flesh creeping,

Of spirits in the web-hung room
   Up above the stable,
Groans, knocking in the gloom,
   The dancing table,

Of demons in the dry well
   That cheep and mutter,
Clanging of an unseen bell,
   Blood choking the gutter,

Of lust frightful, past belief,
   Lurking unforgotten,
Unrestrainable endless grief
   In breasts long rotten.

A song? What laughter or what song
   Can this house remember?
Do flowers and butterflies belong
   To a blind December?

Surgical Ward: Men

Something occurred after the operation
To scare the surgeons (though no fault of theirs),
Whose reassurance did not fool me long.
Beyond the shy, concerned faces of nurses
A single white-hot eye, focusing on me,
Forced sweat in rivers down from scalp to belly.
I whistled, gasped or sang, with blanching knuckles
Clutched at my bed-grip almost till it cracked:
Too proud, still, to let loose Bedlamite screeches
And bring the charge-nurse scuttling down the aisle
With morphia-needle levelled. . . .
                              Lady Morphia—
Her scorpion kiss and dark gyrating dreams—
She in mistrust of whom I dared out-dare,
Two minutes longer than seemed possible,
Pain, that unpurposed, matchless elemental
Stronger than fear, stranger than love.

The Leveller

Near Matinpuisch that night of hell
Two men were struck by the same shell,
Together tumbling in one heap
Senseless and limp like slaughtered sheep.

One was a pale eighteen-year-old,
Blue-eyed and thin and not too bold,
Pressed for the war ten years too soon,
The shame and pity of his platoon.

The other came from far-off lands
With bristling chin and whiskered hands,
He had known death and hell before
In Mexico and Ecuador.

Yet in his death this cut-throat wild
Groaned 'Mother! Mother!' like a child,
While that poor innocent in man's clothes
Died cursing God with brutal oaths.

Old Sergeant Smith, kindest of men,
Wrote out two copies there and then
Of his accustomed funeral speech
To cheer the womenfolk of each:—

'He died a hero's death: and we
His comrades of "A" Company
Deeply regret his death: we shall
All deeply miss so true a pal.'

Recalling War

Entrance and exit wounds are silvered clean,
The track aches only when the rain reminds.
The one-legged man forgets his leg of wood,
The one-armed man his jointed wooden arm.
The blinded man sees with his ears and hands
As much or more than once with both his eyes.
Their war was fought these twenty years ago
And now assumes the nature-look of time,
As when the morning traveller turns and views
His wild night-stumbling carved into a hill.

What, then, was war? No mere discord of flags
But an infection of the common sky
That sagged ominously upon the earth
Even when the season was the airiest May.
Down pressed the sky, and we, oppressed, thrust out
Boastful tongue, clenched fist and valiant yard.
Natural infirmities were out of mode,
For Death was young again: patron alone
Of healthy dying, premature fate-spasm.

Fear made fine bed-fellows. Sick with delight
At life's discovered transitoriness,
Our youth became all-flesh and waived the mind.
Never was such antiqueness of romance,
Such tasty honey oozing from the heart.
And old importances came swimming back—
Wine, meat, log-fires, a roof over the head,
A weapon at the thigh, surgeons at call.
Even there was a use again for God—
A word of rage in lack of meat, wine, fire,
In ache of wounds beyond all surgeoning.

War was return of earth to ugly earth,
War was foundering of sublimities,
Extinction of each happy art and faith
By which the world had still kept head in air,
Protesting logic or protesting love,
Until the unendurable moment struck—
The inward scream, the duty to run mad.

And we recall the merry ways of guns:
Nibbling the walls of factory and church
Like a child, piecrust; felling groves of trees
Like a child, dandelions with a switch.
Machine-guns rattle toy-like from a hill,
Down in a row the brave tin-soldiers fall:
A sight to be recalled in elder days
When learnedly the future we devote
To yet more boastful visions of despair.

The Pier Glass

Lost manor where I walk continually
A ghost, though yet in woman's flesh and blood:
Up your broad stairs mounting with outspread fingers
And gliding steadfast down your corridors
I come by nightly custom to this room,
And even on sultry afternoons I come
Drawn by a thread of time-sunk memory.

Empty, unless for a huge bed of state
Shrouded with rusty curtains drooped awry
(A puppet theatre where malignant fancy
Peoples the wings with fear). At my right hand
A ravelled bell-pull hangs in readiness
To summon me from attic glooms above
Service of elder ghosts; here, at my left,
A sullen pier-glass, cracked from side to side,
Scorns to present the face (as do new mirrors)
With a lying flush, but shows it melancholy
And pale, as faces grow that look in mirrors.

Is there no life, nothing but the thin shadow
And blank foreboding, never a wainscot rat
Rasping a crust? Or at the window-pane
No fly, no bluebottle, no starveling spider?
The windows frame a prospect of cold skies
Half-merged with sea, as at the first creation—
Abstract, confusing welter. Face about,
Peer rather in the glass once more, take note
Of self, the grey lips and long hair dishevelled,
Sleep-staring eyes. Ah, mirror, for Christ's love
Give me one token that there still abides
Remote—beyond this island mystery,
So be it only this side Hope, somewhere,
In streams, on sun-warm mountain pasturage—
True life, natural breath; not this phantasma.

The Face In The Mirror

Grey haunted eyes, absent-mindedly glaring
From wide, uneven orbits; one brow drooping
Somewhat over the eye
Because of a missile fragment still inhering,
Skin deep, as a foolish record of old-world fighting.

Crookedly-broken nose—low tackling caused it;
Cheeks, furrowed; coarse grey hair, flying frenetic;
Forehead, wrinkled and high;
Jowls, prominent; ears, large; jaw, pugilistic;
Teeth, few; lips, full and ruddy; mouth, ascetic.

I pause with razor poised, scowling derision
At the mirrored man whose beard needs my attention,
And once more ask him why
He still stands ready, with a boy's presumption,
To court the queen in her high silk pavilion.

A Slice Of Wedding Cake

Why have such scores of lovely, gifted girls
    Married impossible men?
Simple self-sacrifice may be ruled out,
    And missionary endeavour, nine times out of ten.

Repeat 'impossible men': not merely rustic,
    Foul-tempered or depraved
(Dramatic foils chosen to show the world
    How well women behave, and always have behaved).

Impossible men, : idle, illiterate,
Self-pitying, dirty, sly,
For whose appearance even in City parks
    Excuses must be made to casual passers-by.

Has God's supply of tolerable husbands
    Fallen, in fact, so low?
Or do I always over-value woman
    At the expense of man?
                    Do I?
                            It might be so.

Counting The Beats

You, love, and I,
(He whispers) you and I,
And if no more than only you and I
What care you or I?

Counting the beats,
Counting the slow heart beats,
The bleeding to death of time in slow heart beats,
Wakeful they lie.

Cloudless day,
Night, and a cloudless day;
Yet the huge storm will burst upon their heads one day
From a bitter sky.

Where shall we be,
(She whispers) where shall we be,
When death strikes home, O where then shall we be
Who were you and I?

Not there but here,
(He whispers) only here,
As we are, here, together, now and here,
Always you and I.

Counting the beats,
Counting the slow heart beats,
The bleeding to death of time in slow heart beats,
Wakeful they lie.

Conversation Piece

By moonlight
At midnight,
Under the vines,
A hotel chair .
Settles down moodily before the headlines
Of a still-folded evening newspaper.

The other chair
Of the pair
Lies on its back,
Stiff as in pain,
Having been overturned with an angry crack;
And there till morning, alas, it must remain.

On the terrace
No blood-trace,
No sorry glitter
Of a knife, nothing:
Not even the fine-torn fragments of a letter
Or the dull gleam of a flung-off wedding-ring.

Still stable
On the table
Two long-stemmed glasses,
One full of drink,
Watch how the rat among the vines passes
And how the moon trembles on the crag's brink.

D. H. Lawrence

Piano

Softly, in the dusk, a woman is singing to me;
Taking me back down the vista of years, till I see
 A child sitting under the piano, in the boom of the tingling strings
And pressing the small, poised feet of a mother who smiles as she
sings.

In spite of myself, the insidious mastery of song
Betrays me back, till the heart of me weeps to belong
To the old Sunday evenings at home, with winter outside
And hymns in the cosy parlour, the tinkling piano our guide.

So now it is vain for the singer to burst into clamour
With the great black piano appassionato. The glamour
Of childish days is upon me, my manhood is cast
 Down in the flood of remembrance, I weep like a child for the past.

The Collier's Wife

Somebody's knockin' at th'door
    Mother, come down an' see!
—I's think it's nobbut a beggar;
    Say I'm busy.

It's not a beggar, mother; hark
    How 'ard 'e knocks!
—Eh, tha'rt a mard-arsed kid,
    'E'll gie thee socks!

Shout an' ax what 'e wants,
    I canna come down.
—'E says, is it Arthur Holliday's?
    —Say Yes, tha clown.

37

'E says: Tell your mother as 'er mester's
    Got hurt i' th' pit—
What? Oh my Sirs, 'e never says that,
    That's not it!

Come out o' th' way an' let me see!
    Eh, there's no peace!
An' stop thy scraightin', childt,
    Do shut thy face!

'Your mester's 'ad a accident
    An' they ta'ein' 'im i' th' ambulance
Ter Nottingham.'—Eh dear o' me,
    If 'e's not a man for mischance!

Wheer's 'e hurt this time, lad?
    —I dunna know,
They on'y towd me it wor bad—
    It would be so!

Out o' my way, childt! dear o' me, wheer
    'Ave I put 'is clean stockin's an' shirt?
Goodness knows if they'll be able
    To take off 'is pit-dirt!

An' what a moan 'e'll make! there niver
    Was such a man for a fuss
If anything ailed 'im; at any rate
    I shan't 'ave 'im to nuss.

I do 'ope as it's not so very bad!
    Eh, what a shame it seems
As some should ha'e hardly a smite o' trouble
    An' others 'as reams!

It's a shame as 'e should be knocked about
    Like this, I'm sure it is!
'E's 'ad twenty accidents, if 'e's 'ad one;
    Owt bad, an' it's his!

There's one thing, we s'll 'ave a peaceful 'ouse f'r a bit,
  Thank heaven for a peaceful house!
An' there's compensation, sin' it's accident,
  An' club-money—I won't growse.

An' a fork an' a spoon 'e'll want—an' what else?
  I s'll never catch that train!
What a traipse it is, if a man gets hurt!
  I sh'd think 'e'll get right again.

At The Window

The pine-trees bend to listen to the autumn wind as it mutters
Something which sets the black poplars ashake with hysterical
                                                          laughter;
As slowly the house of day is closing its eastern shutters.

Farther down the valley the clustered tombstones recede,
Winding about their dimness the mist's grey cerements, after
The street-lamps in the twilight have suddenly started to bleed.

The leaves fly over the window, and utter a word as they pass
To the face that gazes outwards, watching for night to waft a
Meaning or a message over the window glass.

Brooding Grief

A yellow leaf, from the darkness
Hops like a frog before me;
Why should I start and stand still?
I was watching the woman that bore me
Stretched in the brindled darkness
Of the sick-room, rigid with will
To die: and the quick leaf tore me
Back to this rainy swill
Of leaves and lamps and the city street mingled before me.

Giorno Dei Morti

Along the avenue of cypresses,
All in their scarlet cloaks and surplices
Of linen, go the chanting choristers,
The priests in gold and black, the villagers. . . .

And all along the path to the cemetery
The round dark heads of men crowd silently,
And black-scarved faces of womenfolk, wistfully
Watch at the banner of death, and the mystery.

And at the foot of a grave a father stands
With sunken head, and forgotten, folded hands;
And at the foot of a grave a mother kneels
With pale shut face, nor either hears nor feels

The coming of the chanting choristers
Between the avenue of cypresses,
The silence of the many villagers,
The candle-flames beside the surplices.

Bat

At evening, sitting on this terrace,
When the sun from the west, beyond Pisa, beyond the mountains
                                                    of Carrara
Departs, and the world is taken by surprise . . .

When the tired flower of Florence is in gloom beneath the glowing
Brown hills surrounding . . .

When under the arches of the Ponte Vecchio
A green light enters against stream, flush from the west,
Against the current of obscure Arno . . .

Look up, and you see things flying
Between the day and the night;
Swallows with spools of dark thread sewing the shadows together.
A circle swoop, and a quick parabola under the bridge arches
Where light pushes through;
A sudden turning upon itself of a thing in the air.
A dip to the water.

And you think:
'The swallows are flying so late!'

Swallows?

Dark air-life looping
Yet missing the pure loop . . .
A twitch, a twitter, an elastic shudder in flight
And serrated wings against the sky,
Like a glove, a black glove thrown up at the light,
And falling back.

Never swallows!
Bats!
The swallows are gone.

At a wavering instant the swallows give way to bats
By the Ponte Vecchio . . .
Changing guard.

Bats, and an uneasy creeping in one's scalp
As the bats swoop overhead!
Flying madly.

Pipistrello!
Black piper on an infinitesimal pipe.
Little lumps that fly in air and have voices indefinite, wildly
vindictive;

Wings like bits of umbrella.

Bats!

Creatures that hang themselves up like an old rag, to sleep;
And disgustingly upside down.
Hanging upside down like rows of disgusting old rags
And grinning in their sleep.
Bats!

In China the bat is symbol of happiness.

Not for me!

Snake

A snake came to my water-trough
On a hot, hot day, and I in pyjamas for the heat,
To drink there.

In the deep, strange-scented shade of the great dark carob-tree
I came down the steps with my pitcher
And must wait, must stand and wait, for there he was at the trough
                                                    before me.

He reached down from a fissure in the earth-wall in the gloom
And trailed his yellow-brown slackness soft-bellied down,
                            over the edge of the stone trough
And rested his throat upon the stone bottom,
And where the water had dripped from the tap, in a small
                                                    clearness,
He sipped with his straight mouth,
Softly drank through his straight gums, into his slack long body,
Silently.

Someone was before me at my water-trough,
And I, like a second comer, waiting.

He lifted his head from his drinking, as cattle do,
And looked at me vaguely, as drinking cattle do,
And flickered his two-forked tongue from his lips, and mused a
                                                    moment,
And stooped and drank a little more,
Being earth-brown, earth-golden from the burning bowels of the
                                                    earth
On the day of Sicilian July, with Etna smoking.

The voice of my education said to me
He must be killed,
For in Sicily the black, black snakes are innocent, the gold are
                                                    venomous.

And voices in me said, If you were a man
You would take a stick and break him now, and finish him off.

But must I confess how I liked him,
How glad I was he had come like a guest in quiet, to drink at my
water-trough
And depart peaceful, pacified, and thankless,
Into the burning bowels of this earth?

Was it cowardice, that I dared not kill him?
Was it perversity, that I longed to talk to him?
Was it humility, to feel so honoured?
I felt so honoured.

And yet those voices:
If you were not afraid, you would kill him!

And truly I was afraid, I was most afraid,
But even so, honoured still more
That he should seek my hospitality
From out the dark door of the secret earth.

He drank enough
And lifted his head, dreamily, as one who has drunken,
And flickered his tongue like a forked night on the air, so black,
Seeming to lick his lips,
And looked around like a god, unseeing, into the air,
And slowly turned his head,
And slowly, very slowly, as if thrice adream,
Proceeded to draw his slow length curving round
And climb again the broken bank of my wall-face.

And as he put his head into that dreadful hole,
And as he slowly drew up, snake-easing his shoulders, and entered
farther,
A sort of horror, a sort of protest against his withdrawing into that
horrid black hole,
Deliberately going into the blackness, and slowly drawing himself
after,
Overcame me now his back was turned.

I looked round, I put down my pitcher,
I picked up a clumsy log
And threw it at the water-trough with a clatter.

I think it did not hit him,
But suddenly that part of him that was left behind convulsed in
                                        undignified haste,
Writhed like lighting, and was gone
Into the black hole, the earth-lipped fissure in the wall-front,
At which, in the intense still noon, I stared with fascination.

And immediately I regretted it.
I thought how paltry, how vulgar, what a mean act!
I despised myself and the voices of my accursed human education.

And I thought of the albatross,
And I wished he would come back, my snake.

For he seemed to me again like a king,
Like a king in exile, uncrowned in the underworld,
Now due to be crowned again.

And so, I missed my chance with one of the lords
Of life.
And I have something to expiate;
A pettiness.

Kangaroo

In the northern hemisphere
Life seems to leap at the air, or skim under the wind
Like stags on rocky ground, or pawing horses, or springy scut-
                                        tailed rabbits.

Or else rush horizontal to charge at the sky's horizon,
Like bulls or bisons or wild pigs.

Or slip like water slippery towards its ends,
As foxes, stoats, and wolves, and prairie dogs.

Only mice, and moles, and rats, and badgers, and beavers, and
                                        perhaps bears
Seem belly-plumbed to the earth's mid-navel.
Or frogs that when they leap come flop, and flop to the centre of
                                        the earth.

44

But the yellow antipodal Kangaroo, when she sits up,
Who can unseat her, like a liquid drop that is heavy, and just
           touches earth.

The downward drip
The down-urge.
So much denser than cold-blooded frogs.

Delicate mother Kangaroo
Sitting up there rabbit-wise, but huge, plumb-weighted,
And lifting her beautiful slender face, oh! so much more gently
     and finely lined than a rabbit's, or than a hare's,
Lifting her face to nibble at a round white peppermint drop, which
       she loves, sensitive mother Kangaroo.

Her sensitive, long, pure-bred face.
Her full antipodal eyes, so dark,
So big and quiet and remote, having watched so many empty
         dawns in silent Australia.

Her little loose hands, and drooping Victorian shoulders.
And then her great weight below the waist, her vast pale belly
With a thin young yellow little paw hanging out, and straggle of a
        long thin ear, like ribbon,
Like a funny trimming to the middle of her belly, thin little dangle
       of an immature paw, and one thin ear.

Her belly, her big haunches
And, in addition, the great muscular python-stretch of her tail.

There, she shan't have any more peppermint drops.
So she wistfully, sensitively sniffs the air, and then turns, goes off in
         slow sad leaps

On the long flat skis of her legs,
Steered and propelled by that steel-strong snake of a tail.

Stops again, half turns, inquisitive to look back.
While something stirs quickly in her belly, and a lean little face
        comes out, as from a window,

Peaked and a bit dismayed,
Only to disappear again quickly away from the sight of the world,
                                to snuggle down in the warmth,
Leaving the trail of a different paw hanging out.

Still she watches with eternal, cocked wistfulness!
How full her eyes are, like the full, fathomless, shining eyes of an
                                Australian black-boy
Who has been lost so many centuries on the margins of existence!

She watches with insatiable wistfulness.
Untold centuries of watching for something to come,
For a new signal from life, in that silent lost land of the South.

Where nothing bites but insects and snakes and the sun, small life.
Where no bull roared, no cow ever lowed, no stag cried, no
                leopard screeched, no lion coughed, no dog barked,
But all was silent save for parrots occasionally, in the haunted blue
                                bush.

Wistfully watching, with wonderful liquid eyes.
And all her weight, all her blood, dripping sack-wise down
                                towards the earth's centre,
And the live little-one taking in its paw at the door of her belly.

Leap then, and come down on the line that draws to the earth's
                                deep, heavy centre.

Humming-Bird

I can imagine, in some otherworld
Primeval-dumb, far back
In that most awful stillness, that only gasped and hummed,
Humming-birds raced down the avenues.

Before anything had a soul,
While life was a heave of Matter, half inanimate,
This little bit chipped off in brilliance
And went whizzing through the slow, vast, succulent stems.

I believe there were no flowers then,
In the world where the humming-bird flashed ahead of creation.
I believe he pierced the slow vegetable veins with his long beak.

46

Probably he was big
As mosses, and little lizards, they say, were once big.
Probably he was a jabbing, terrifying monster.

We look at him through the wrong end of the long telescope of
                                                                Time,
Luckily for us.

Bavarian Gentians

Not every man has gentians in his house
in Soft September, at slow, Sad Michaelmas.

Bavarian gentians, big and dark, only dark
darkening the day-time torch-like with the smoking blueness of
                                                    Pluto's gloom,
ribbed and torch-like, with their blaze of darkness spread blue
down flattening into points, flattened under the sweep of white day
torch-flower of the blue-smoking darkness, Pluto's dark-blue
                                                                daze,
black lamps from the halls of Dis, burning dark blue,
giving off darkness, blue darkness, as Demeter's pale lamps give off
                                                                light,
lead me then, lead me the way.

Reach me a gentian, give me a torch
let me guide myself with the blue, forked torch of this flower
down the darker and darker stairs, where blue is darkened on
                                                        blueness;
even where Persephone goes, just now, from the frosted September
to the sightless realm where darkness is awake upon the dark
and Persephone herself is but a voice
or a darkness invisible enfolded in the deeper dark
of the arms Plutonic, and pierced with the passion of dense gloom,
among the splendour of torches of darkness, shedding darkness on
                            the lost bride and her groom.

Work

There is no point in work
unless it absorbs you
like an absorbing game.

If it doesn't absorb you
if it's never any fun,
don't do it.

When a man goes out into his work
he is alive like a tree in spring,
he is living, not merely working.

When the Hindus weave thin wool into long, long lengths of stuff
with their thin dark hands and their wide dark eyes and their still
                                                        souls absorbed
they are like slender trees putting forth leaves, a long white web of
                                                        living leaf,
the tissue they weave,
and they clothe themselves in white as a tree clothes itself in its own
                                                        foliage.

As with cloth, so with houses, ships, shoes, wagons or cups or
                                                        loaves
men might put them forth as a snail its shell, as a bird that leans
its breast against its nest, to make it round,
as the turnip models his round root, as the bush makes flowers and
                                                        gooseberries,
putting them forth, not manufacturing them,
and cities might be as once they were, bowers grown out from the
                                                        busy bodies of people.

And so it will be again, men will smash the machines.

At last, for the sake of clothing himself in his own leaf-like cloth
tissued from his life,
and dwelling in his own bowery house, like a beaver's nibbled
                                                        mansion
and drinking from cups that came off his fingers like flowers off
                                                        their five-fold stem,
he will cancel the machines we have got.

Money-Madness

Money is our madness, our vast collective madness.

And of course, if the multitude is mad
the individual carries his own grain of insanity around with him.

I doubt if any man living hands out a pound note without a pang;
and a real tremor, if he hands out a ten-pound note.

We quail, money makes us quail.
It has got us down, we grovel before it in strange terror.
And no wonder, for money has a fearful cruel power among men.

But it is not money we are so terrified of,
it is the collective money-madness of mankind.
For mankind says with one voice: How much is he worth?
Has he no money? Then let him eat dirt, and go cold.—

And if I have no money, they will give me a little bread
so I do not die,
but they will make me eat dirt with it.
I shall have to eat dirt, I shall have to eat dirt
if I have no money.

It is that that I am frightened of.
And that fear can become a delirium.
It is fear of my money-mad fellow-men.

We must have some money
to save us from eating dirt.

And this is all wrong.

Bread should be free,
shelter should be free,
fire should be free
to all and anybody, all and anybody, all over the world.

We must regain our sanity about money
before we start killing one another about it.
It's one thing or the other.

W. H. Auden

Night Mail

I

This is the Night Mail crossing the Border,
Bringing the cheque and the postal order,

Letters for the rich, letters for the poor,
The shop at the corner, the girl next door.

Pulling up Beattock, a steady climb:
The gradient's against her, but she's on time.

Past cotton-grass and moorland boulder,
Shovelling white steam over her shoulder,

Snorting noisily, she passes
Silent miles of wind-bent grasses.

Birds turn their heads as she approaches,
Stare from bushes at her blank-faced coaches.

Sheep-dogs cannot turn her course;
They slumber on with paws across.

In the farm she passes no one wakes,
But a jug in a bedroom gently shakes.

II

Dawn freshens. Her climb is done.
Down towards Glasgow she descends,
Towards the steam tugs yelping down a glade of cranes,
Towards the fields of apparatus, the furnaces
Set on the dark plain like gigantic chessmen.
All Scotland waits for her:
In dark glens, beside pale-green lochs,
Men long for news.

III

Letters of thanks, letters from banks,
Letters of joy from girl and boy,
Receipted bills and invitations
To inspect new stock or to visit relations,
And applications for situations,
And timid lovers' declarations,
And gossip, gossip from all the nations,
News circumstantial, news financial,
Letters with holiday snaps to enlarge in,
Letters with faces scrawled on the margin,
Letters from uncles, cousins and aunts,
Letters to Scotland from the South of France,
Letters of condolence to Highlands and Lowlands,
Written on paper of every hue,
The pink, the violet, the white and the blue,
The chatty, the catty, the boring, the adoring,
The cold and official and the heart's outpouring,
Clever, stupid, short and long,
The typed and the printed and the spelt all wrong.

IV

Thousands are still asleep,
Dreaming of terrifying monsters
Or a friendly tea beside the band in Cranston's or Crawford's:
Asleep in working Glasgow, asleep in well-set Edinburgh,
Asleep in granite Aberdeen,
They continue their dreams,
But shall wake soon and hope for letters,
And none will hear the postman's knock
Without a quickening of the heart.
For who can bear to feel himself forgotten?

No Change Of Place

Who will endure
Heat of day and winter danger,
Journey from one place to another,
Nor be content to lie
Till evening upon headland over bay,
Between the land and sea
Or smoking wait till hour of food,
Leaning on chained-up gate
At edge of wood?

Metals run,
Burnished or rusty in the sun,
From town to town,
And signals all along are down;
Yet nothing passes
But envelopes between these places,
Snatched at the gate and panting read indoors,
And first spring flowers arriving smashed,
Disaster stammered over wires,
And pity flashed.

For should professional traveller come,
Asked at the fireside, he is dumb,
Declining with a secret smile,
And all the while
Conjectures on our maps grow stranger
And threaten danger.

There is no change of place:
No one will ever know
For what conversion brilliant capital is waiting,
What ugly feast may village band be celebrating;
For no one goes
Further than railhead or the ends of piers,
Will neither go nor send his son
Further through foothills than the rotting stack
Where gaitered gamekeeper with dog and gun
Will shout 'Turn back'.

From Ode

Though aware of our rank and alert to obey orders,
Watching with binoculars the movement of the grass for an
                                                  ambush,
The pistol cocked, the code-word committed to memory;
        The youngest drummer
Knows all the peace-time stories like the oldest soldier,
        Though frontier-conscious,

About the tall white gods who landed from their open boat,
Skilled in the working of copper, appointing our feast-days,
Before the islands were submerged, when the weather was calm,
        The maned lion common,
An open wishing-well in every garden;
        When love came easy.

Perfectly certain, all of us, but not from the records,
Not from the unshaven agent who returned to the camp:
The pillar dug from the desert recorded only
        The sack of a city,
The agent clutching his side collapsed at our feet,
        'Sorry! They got me!'

Yes, they were living here once but do not now,
Yes, they are living still but do not here;
Lying awake after Lights Out a recruit may speak up:
        'Who told you all this?'
The tent-talk pauses a little till a veteran answers
        'Go to sleep, Sonny!'

Turning over he closes his eyes, and then in a moment
Sees the sun at midnight bright over cornfield and pasture,
Our hope. . . . Someone jostles him, fumbling for boots,
        Time to change guard:
Boy, the quarrel was before your time, the aggressor
        No one you know.

Embassy

As evening fell the day's oppression lifted;
Far peaks came into focus; it had rained:
Across wide lawns and cultured flowers drifted
The conversation of the highly trained.

Two gardeners watched them pass and priced their shoes;
A chauffeur waited, reading in the drive,
For them to finish their exchange of views:
It seemed a picture of the private life.

Far off, no matter what good they intended,
The armies waited for a verbal error
With all the instruments for causing pain:

And on the issue of their charm depended
A land laid waste, with all its young men slain,
Its women weeping, and its towns in terror.

O What Is That Sound

O what is that sound which so thrills the ear
    Down in the valley drumming, drumming?
Only the scarlet soldiers, dear,
    The soldiers coming.

O what is that light I see flashing so clear
    Over the distance brightly, brightly?
Only the sun on their weapons, dear,
    As they step lightly.

O what are they doing with all that gear,
    What are they doing this morning, this morning?
Only their usual manoeuvres, dear,
    Or perhaps a warning.

O why have they left the road down there,
    Why are they suddenly wheeling, wheeling?
Perhaps a change in their orders, dear.
    Why are you kneeling?

O haven't they stopped for the doctor's care,
　　Haven't they reined their horses, their horses?
Why, they are none of them wounded, dear,
　　None of these forces.

O is it the parson they want, with white hair,
　　Is it the parson, is it, is it?
No, they are passing his gateway, dear,
　　Without a visit.

O it must be the farmer who lives so near.
　　It must be the farmer so cunning, so cunning?
They have passed the farmyard already, dear,
　　And now they are running.

O where are you going? Stay with me here!
　　Were the vows you swore deceiving, deceiving?
No, I promised to love you, dear,
　　But I must be leaving.

O it's broken the lock and splintered the door,
　　O it's the gate where they're turning, turning;
Their boots are heavy on the floor
　　And their eyes are burning.

Refugee Blues

Say this city has ten million souls,
Some are living in mansions, some are living in holes:
Yet there's no place for us, my dear, yet there's no place for us.

Once we had a country and we thought it was fair,
Look in the atlas and you'll find it there:
We cannot go there now, my dear, we cannot go there now.

In the village churchyard there grows an old yew,
Every spring it blossoms anew:
Old passports can't do that, my dear, old passports can't do that.

The consul banged the table and said:
'If you've got no passport you're officially dead':
But we are still alive, my dear, but we are still alive.

Went to a committee; they offered me a chair;
Asked me politely to return next year:
But where shall we go to-day, my dear, but where shall we go to-
day?

Came to a public meeting; the speaker got up and said:
'If we let them in, they will steal our daily bread';
He was talking of you and me, my dear, he was talking of you and
me.

Thought I heard the thunder rumbling in the sky;
It was Hitler over Europe, saying: 'They must die';
We were in his mind, my dear, we were in his mind.

Saw a poodle in a jacket fastened with a pin,
Saw a door opened and a cat let in:
But they weren't German Jews, my dear, but they weren't German
Jews.

Went down the harbour and stood upon the quay,
Saw the fish swimming as if they were free:
Only ten feet away, my dear, only ten feet away.

Walked through a wood, saw the birds in the trees;
They had no politicians and sang at their ease:
They weren't the human race, my dear, they weren't the human
race.

Dreamt I saw a building with a thousand floors,
A thousand windows and a thousand doors;
Not one of them was ours, my dear, not one of them was ours.

Stood on a great plain in the falling snow;
Ten thousand soldiers marched to and fro:
Looking for you and me, my dear, looking for you and me.

Epitaph On A Tyrant

Perfection, of a kind, was what he was after,
And the poetry he invented was easy to understand;
He knew human folly like the back of his hand,
And was greatly interested in armies and fleets;
When he laughed, respectable senators burst with laughter,
And when he cried the little children died in the streets.

Surgical Ward

They are and suffer; that is all they do:
A bandage hides the place where each is living,
His knowledge of the world restricted to
The treatment that the instruments are giving.

And lie apart like epochs from each other
—Truth in their sense is how much they can bear;
It is not talk like ours, but groans they smother—
And are remote as plants; we stand elsewhere.

For who when healthy can become a foot?
Even a scratch we can't recall when cured,
But are boist'rous in a moment and believe

In the common world of the uninjured, and cannot
Imagine isolation. Only happiness is shared,
And anger, and the idea of love.

Musée Des Beaux Arts

About suffering they were never wrong,
The Old Masters: how well they understood
Its human position; how it takes place
While someone else is eating or opening a window or just walking
                                                    dully along;
How, when the aged are reverently, passionately waiting
For the miraculous birth, there always must be
Children who did not specially want it to happen, skating
On a pond at the edge of the wood:

They never forgot
That even the dreadful martyrdom must run its course
Anyhow in a corner, some untidy spot
Where the dogs go on with their doggy life and the torturer's horse
Scratches its innocent behind on a tree.

In Brueghel's *Icarus*, for instance: how everything turns away
Quite leisurely from the disaster; the ploughman may
Have heard the splash, the forsaken cry,
But for him it was not an important failure; the sun shone
As it had to on the white legs disappearing into the green
Water; and the expensive delicate ship that must have seen
Something amazing, a boy falling out of the sky,
Had somewhere to get to and sailed calmly on.

The Unknown Citizen

(To JS/o7/M/378
This Marble Monument
Is Erected by the State)

He was found by the Bureau of Statistics to be
One against whom there was no official complaint,
And all the reports on his conduct agree
That, in the modern sense of an old-fashioned word, he was a
                                                        saint,
For in everything he did he served the Greater Community.
Except for the War till the day he retired
He worked in a factory and never got fired,
But satisfied his employers, Fudge Motors Inc.
Yet he wasn't a scab or odd in his views,
For his Union reports that he paid his dues,
(Our report on his Union shows it was sound)
And our Social Psychology workers found
That he was popular with his mates and liked a drink.
The Press are convinced that he bought a paper every day
And that his reactions to advertisements were normal in every way.
Policies taken out in his name prove that he was fully insured,
And his Health-card shows he was once in hospital but left it cured.
Both Producers Research and High-Grade Living declare
He was fully sensible to the advantages of the Instalment Plan
And had everything necessary to the Modern Man,
A phonograph, a radio, a car and frigidaire.

Our researchers into Public Opinion are content
That he held the proper opinions for the time of year;
When there was peace, he was for peace; when there was war, he
went.
He was married and added five children to the population,
Which our Eugenist says was the right number for a parent of his
generation,
And our teachers report that he never interfered with their
education.
Was he free? Was he happy? The question is absurd:
Had anything been wrong, we should certainly have heard.

As I Walked Out One Evening

As I walked out one evening,
  Walking down Bristol Street,
The crowds upon the pavement
  Were fields of harvest wheat.

And down by the brimming river
  I heard a lover sing
Under an arch of the railway:
  'Love has no ending.

'I'll love you, dear, I'll love you
  Till China and Africa meet,
And the river jumps over the mountain
  And the salmon sing in the street,

'I'll love you till the ocean
  Is folded and hung up to dry
And the seven stars go squawking
  Like geese about the sky.

The years shall run like rabbits,
  For in my arms I hold
The Flower of the Ages,
  And the first love of the world.'

But all the clocks in the city
  Began to whirr and chime:
'O let not Time deceive you,
  You cannot conquer Time.

'In the burrows of the Nightmare
    Where Justice naked is,
Time watches from the shadow
    And coughs when you would kiss.

'In headaches and in worry
    Vaguely life leaks away,
And Time will have his fancy
    To-morrow or to-day.

'Into many a green valley
    Drifts the appalling snow;
Time breaks the threaded dances
    And the diver's brilliant bow.

'O plunge your hands in water,
    Plunge them in up to the wrist;
Stare, stare in the basin
    And wonder what you've missed.

'The glacier knocks in the cupboard,
    The desert sighs in the bed,
And the crack in the tea-cup opens
    A lane to the land of the dead.

'Where the beggars raffle the banknotes
    And the Giant is enchanting to Jack,
And the Lily-white Boy is a Roarer,
    And Jill goes down on her back.

'O look, look in the mirror,
    O look in your distress;
Life remains a blessing
    Although you cannot bless.

'O stand, stand at the window
    As the tears scald and start;
You shall love your crooked neighbour
    With your crooked heart.'

It was late, late in the evening
    The lovers they were gone;
The clocks had ceased their chiming,
    And the deep river ran on.

Our Bias

The hour-glass whispers to the lion's roar,
The clock-towers tell the gardens day and night,
How many errors Time has patience for,
How wrong they are in being always right.

Yet Time, however loud its chimes or deep,
However fast its falling torrent flows,
Has never put one lion off its leap
Nor shaken the assurance of a rose.

For they, it seems, care only for success:
While we choose words according to their sound
And judge a problem by its awkwardness;

And Time with us was always popular.
When have we not preferred some going round
To going straight to where we are?

If I Could Tell You

Time will say nothing but I told you so,
Time only knows the price we have to pay;
If I could tell I would let you know.

If we should weep when clowns put on their show,
If we should stumble when musicians play,
Time will say nothing but I told you so.

There are no fortunes to be told, although,
Because I love you more than I can say,
If I could tell you I would let you know.

The winds must come from somewhere when they blow,
There must be reasons why the leaves decay;
Time will say nothing but I told you so.

Perhaps the roses really want to grow,
The vision seriously intends to stay;
If I could tell you I would let you know.

Suppose the lions all get up and go,
And all the brooks and soldiers run away;
Will Time say nothing but I told you so?
If I could tell you I would let you know.

Seascape

Look, stranger, on this island now
The leaping light for your delight discovers,
Stand stable here
And silent be,
That through the channels of the ear
May wander like a river
The swaying sound of the sea.

Here at a small field's ending pause
When the chalk wall falls to the foam and its tall ledges
Oppose the pluck
And knock of the tide,
And the shingle scrambles after the suck-
-ing surf,
And a gull lodges
A moment on its sheer side.

Far off like floating seeds the ships
Diverge on urgent voluntary errands,
And this full view
Indeed may enter
And move in memory as now these clouds do,
That pass the harbour mirror
And all the summer through the water saunter.

Louis Macneice

Autobiography

In my childhood trees were green
And there was plenty to be seen.

Come back early or never come.

My father made the walls resound,
He wore his collar the wrong way round.

Come back early or never come.

My mother wore a yellow dress;
Gently, gently, gentleness.

Come back early or never come.

When I was five the black dreams came;
Nothing after was quite the same.

Come back early or never come.

The dark was talking to the dead;
The lamp was dark beside my bed.

Come back early or never come.

When I woke they did not care;
Nobody, nobody was there.

Come back early or never come.

When my silent terror cried,
Nobody, nobody replied.

Come back early or never come.

I got up; the chilly sun
Saw me walk away alone.

Come back early or never come.

Soap Suds

This brand of soap has the same smell as once in the big
House he visited when he was eight: the walls of the bathroom
                        open
To reveal a lawn where a great yellow ball rolls back through a
                        hoop
To rest at the head of a mallet held in the hands of a child.

And these were the joys of that house: a tower with a telescope;
Two great faded globes, one of the earth, one of the stars;
A stuffed black dog in the hall; a walled garden with bees;
A rabbit warren; a rockery; a vine under glass; the sea.

To which he has now returned. The day of course is fine
And a grown-up voice cries Play! The mallet slowly swings,
Then crack, a great gong booms from the dog-dark hall and the
                        ball
Skims forward through the hoop and then through the next and
                        then

Through hoops where no hoops were and each dissolves in turn
And the grass has grown head-high and an angry voice cries Play!
But the ball is lost and the mallet slipped long since from the hands
Under the running tap that are not the hands of a child.

Solstice

How did midsummer come so soon,
The lean trees racing into lush?
He had turned his back one moment, then turned
And took it full in the face—the gush
Of green, the stare of blue, the sieve
Of sun and shadow, the wish to live.

And what was nowhere now was here
And here was all and all was good;
Between the lines the words were strange
Yet not to be misunderstood.
The glad flowers talked with tongues of flame
And who was he was not the same.

Nor was there question who was she
For whom his years were blessed to wait,
Whose opening eyes to him were now,
As his to hers, an open gate,
One entrance to one constant song.
How can midsummer stay so long?

Snow

The room was suddenly rich and the great bay-window was
Spawning snow and pink roses against it
Soundlessly collateral and incompatible:
World is suddener than we fancy it.

World is crazier and more of it than we think,
Incorrigibly plural. I peel and portion
A tangerine and spit the pips and feel
The drunkenness of things being various.

And the fire flames with a bubbling sound for world
Is more spiteful and gay than one supposes—
On the tongue on the eyes on the ears in the palms of one's
                                                    hands—
There is more than glass between the snow and the huge roses.

The Sunlight On The Garden

The sunlight on the garden
Hardens and grows cold,
We cannot cage the minute
Within its nets of gold,
When all is told
We cannot beg for pardon.

Our freedom as free lances
Advances towards its end;
The earth compels, upon it
Sonnets and birds descend;
And soon, my friend,
We shall have no time for dances.

The sky was good for flying
Defying the church bells
And every evil iron
Siren and what it tells:
The earth compels,
We are dying, Egypt, dying

And not expecting pardon,
Hardened in heart anew,
But glad to have sat under
Thunder and rain with you,
And grateful too
For sunlight on the garden.

Les Sylphides

Life in a day: he took his girl to the ballet;
Being shortsighted himself could hardly see it—
    The white skirts in the grey
    Glade and the swell of the music
    Lifting the white sails.

Calyx upon calyx, canterbury bells in the breeze
The flowers on the left mirror to the flowers on the right
    And the naked arms above
    The powdered faces moving
    Like seaweed in a pool.

Now, he thought, we are floating—ageless, oarless—
Now there is no separation, from now on
    You will be wearing white
    Satin and a red sash
    Under the waltzing trees.

But the music stopped, the dancers took their curtain,
The river had come to a lock—a shuffle of programmes—
    And we cannot continue down
    Stream unless we are ready
    To enter the lock and drop.

So they were married—to be the more together—
And found they were never again so much together,
   Divided by the morning tea,
   By the evening paper,
   By children and tradesmen's bills.

Waking at times in the night she found assurance
Due to his regular breathing but wondered whether
   It was really worth it and where
   The river had flowed away
   And where were the white flowers.

Order To View

It was a big house, bleak;
Grass on the drive;
We had been there before
But memory, weak in front of
A blistered door, could find
Nothing alive now;
The shrubbery dripped, a crypt
Of leafmould dreams; a tarnished
Arrow over an empty stable
Shifted a little in the tenuous wind,

And wishes were unable
To rise; on the garden wall
The pear trees had come loose
From rotten loops; one wish,
A rainbow bubble, rose,
Faltered, broke in the dull
Air—What was the use?
The bell-pull would not pull
And the whole place, one might
Have supposed, was deadly ill:
The world was closed,

And remained closed until
A sudden angry tree
Shook itself like a setter
Flouncing out of a pond
And beyond the sombre line
Of limes a cavalcade
Of clouds rose like a shout of
Defiance. Near at hand
Somewhere in a loose-box
A horse neighed
And all the curtains flew out of
The windows; the world was open.

Débâcle

They had built it up—but not for this the lean
And divinatory years,
The red-eyed pioneers
Facing the dark and making the desert green.

Not for this the pale inventor's lamp
Alight till dawn, the hands
Weary with sifting sands,
The burst of nuggets on the miners' camp.

Vision and sinew made it of light and stone;
Not grateful nor enchanted
Their heirs took it for granted
Having a world—a world that was all their own.

At sundown now the windows had gone gold
For half an hour; a quick
Chill came off the brick
Walls and the flesh was suddenly old and cold.

Crumbling between the fingers, under the feet,
Crumbling behind the eyes,
Their world gives way and dies
And something twangs and breaks at the end of the street.

Prayer Before Birth

I am not yet born; O hear me.
Let not the bloodsucking bat or the rat or the stoat or the club-
    footed ghoul come near me.

I am not yet born, console me.
I fear that the human race may with tall walls wall me,
    with strong drugs dope me, with wise lies lure me,
        on black racks rack me, in blood-baths roll me.

I am not yet born; provide me
With water to dandle me, grass to grow for me, trees to talk
    to me, sky to sing to me, birds and a white light
        in the back of my mind to guide me.

I am not yet born; forgive me
For the sins that in me the world shall commit, my words
    when they speak me, my thoughts when they think me,
        my treason engendered by traitors beyond me,
            my life when they murder by means of my
                hands, my death when they live me.

I am not yet born; rehearse me
In the parts I must play and the cues I must take when
    old men lecture me, bureaucrats hector me, mountains
        frown at me, lovers laugh at me, the white
            waves call me to folly and the desert calls
                me to doom and the beggar refuses
                    my gift and my children curse me.

I am not yet born; O hear me,
Let not the man who is beast or who thinks he is God
    come near me.

I am not yet born; O fill me
With strength against those who would freeze my
    humanity, would dragoon me into a lethal automaton,
      would make me a cog in a machine, a thing with
        one face, a thing, and against all those
          who would dissipate my entirety, would
            blow me like thistledown hither and
              thither or hither and thither
                like water held in the
                  hands would spill me.

Let them not make me a stone and let them not spill me.
Otherwise kill me.

Cradle Song For Eleanor

Sleep, my darling, sleep;
    The pity of it all
Is all we compass if
    We watch disaster fall.
Put off your twenty-odd
    Encumbered years and creep
Into the only heaven,
    The robbers' cave of sleep.

The wild grass will whisper,
    Lights of passing cars
Will streak across your dreams
    And fumble at the stars;
Life will tap the window
    Only too soon again,
Life will have her answer—
    Do not ask her when.

When the winsome bubble
    Shivers, when the bough
Breaks, will be the moment
    But not here or now.
Sleep and, asleep, forget
    The watchers on the wall
Awake all night who know
    The pity of it all.

After The Crash

When he came to he knew
Time must have passed because
The asphalt was high with hemlock
Through which he crawled to his crash
Helmet and found it no more
Than his wrinkled hand what it was.

Yet life seemed still going on:
He could hear the signals bounce
Back from the moon and the hens
Fire themselves black in the batteries
And the silence of small blind cats
Debating whether to pounce.

Then he looked up and marked
The gigantic scales in the sky,
The pan on the left dead empty
And the pan on the right dead empty,
And knew in the dead, dead calm
It was too late to die.

Budgie

The budgerigar is baby blue,
Its mirror is rimmed with baby pink,
Its cage is a stage, its perks are props,
Its eyes black pins in a cushionette,
Its tail a needle on a missing disc,
Its voice a small I Am. Beyond
These wires there might be something different—
Galaxy on galaxy, star on star,
Planet on planet, asteroid on asteroid,
Or even those four far walls of the sitting room—
But for all this small blue bundle could bother
Its beak, there is only itself and the universe,
The small blue universe, so *Let me attitudinize,*
Let me attitudinize, let me attitudinize,
For all the world is a stage is a cage
A hermitage a fashion show a crèche an auditorium
Or possibly a space ship. *Earth, can you hear me?*

73

Blue for Budgie calling Me for Mirror:
Budgie, can you hear me? The long tail oscillates,
The mirror jerks in the weightless cage:
Budgie, can you see me? The radio telescope
Picks up a quite different signal, the human
Race recedes and dwindles, the giant
Reptiles cackle in their graves, the mountain
Gorillas exchange their final messages,
But the budgerigar was not born for nothing,
He stands at his post on the burning perch—
I twitter Am—and peeps like a television
Actor admiring himself in the monitor.

The Gardener

He was not able to read or write,
He did odd jobs on gentlemen's places
Cutting the hedge or hoeing the drive
With the smile of a saint,
With the pride of a feudal chief,
For he was not quite all there.

Crippled by rheumatism
By the time his hair was white,
He would reach the garden by twelve
His legs in soiled puttees,
A clay pipe in his teeth,
A tiny flag in his cap,
A white cat behind him,
And his eyes a cornflower blue.

And between the clack of the shears
Or the honing of the scythe
Or the rattle of the rake on the gravel
He would talk to amuse the children,
He would talk to himself or the cat
Or the robin waiting for worms
Perched on the handle of the spade;
Would remember snatches of verse
From the elementary school
About a bee and a wasp
Or the cat by the barndoor spinning;

74

And would talk about himself for ever—
You would never find his like—
Always in the third person;
And would level his stick like a gun
(With a glint in his eye)
Saying "Now I'm a Frenchman"—
He was not quite right in the head.

He believed in God—
The Good Fellow Up There—
And he used a simile of Homer
Watching the falling leaves,
And every year he waited for the Twelfth of July,
Cherishing his sash and his fife
For the carnival of banners and drums.
He was always claiming but never
Obtaining his old age pension,
For he did not know his age.

And his rheumatism at last
Kept him out of the processions.
And he came to work in the garden
Later and later in the day,
Leaving later at night;
In the damp dark of the night
At ten o'clock or later
You could hear him mowing the lawn,
The mower moving forward,
And backward, forward and backward
For he mowed while standing still;
He was not quite up to the job.

But he took a pride in the job,
He kept a bowl of cold
Tea in the crotch of a tree,
Always enjoyed his food
And enjoyed honing the scythe
And making the potato drills
And putting the peasticks in;
And enjoyed the noise of the corncrake,
And the early hawthorn hedge
Peppered black and green,
And the cut grass dancing in the air—
Happy as the day was long.

Till his last sickness took him
And he could not leave his house
And his eyes lost their colour
And he sat by the little range
With a finch in a cage and a framed
Certificate of admission
Into the Orange Order,
And his speech began to wander
And memory ebbed
Leaving upon the shore
Odd shells and heads of wrack
And his soul went out on the ebbing
Tide in a trim boat
To find the Walls of Derry
Or the land of the Ever Young.

The Wiper

Through purblind night the wiper
Reaps a swathe of water
On the screen; we shudder on
    And hardly hold the road,
All we can see a segment
Of blackly shining asphalt
With the wiper moving across it
    Clearing, blurring, clearing.

But what to say of the road?
The monotony of its hardly
Visible camber, the mystery
    Of its far invisible margins,
Will these be always with us,
The night being broken only
By lights that pass or meet us
    From others in moving boxes?

Boxes of glass and water,
Upholstered, equipped with dials
Professing to tell the distance
    We have gone, the speed we are going,
But never a gauge nor needle
To tell us where we are going
Or when day will come, supposing
    This road exists in daytime.

For now we cannot remember
Where we were when it was not
Night, when it was not raining,
    Before this car moved forward
And the wiper backward and forward
Lighting so little before us
Of a road that, crouching forward,
    We watch move always towards us,

Which through the tiny segment
Cleared and blurred by the wiper
Is sucked in under the axle
    To be spewed behind us and lost
While we, dazzled by darkness,
Haul the black future towards us
Peeling the skin from our hands;
    And yet we hold the road.

John Betjeman

Pot Pourri From A Surrey Garden

Miles of pram in the wind and Pam in the gorse track,
  Coco-nut smell of the broom, and a packet of Weights
Press'd in the sand. The thud of a hoof on a horse-track—
    A horse-riding horse for a horse-track—
    Conifer county of Surrey approached
Through remarkable wrought-iron gates.

Over your boundary now, I wash my face in a bird-bath,
  Then which path shall I take? that over there by the pram?
Down by the pond! or—yes, I will take the slippery third path,
    Trodden away with gym shoes,
    Beautiful fir-dry alley that leads
To the bountiful body of Pam.

Pam, I adore you, Pam, you great big mountainous sports girl,
  Whizzing them over the net, full of the strength of five:
That old Malvernian brother, you zephyr and khaki shorts girl,
    Although he's playing for Woking,
    Can't stand up
To your wonderful backhand drive.

See the strength of her arm, as firm and hairy as Hendren's;
  See the size of her thighs, the pout of her lips as, cross,
And full of pent-up strength, she swipes at the rhododendrons,
    Lucky the rhododendrons,
    And flings her arrogant love-lock
Back with a petulant toss.

Over the redolent pinewoods, in at the bathroom casement,
  One fine Saturday, Windlesham bells shall call:
Up the Butterfield aisle rich with Gothic enlacement,
    Licensed now for embracement,
    Pam and I, as the organ
Thunders over you all.

A Subaltern's Love-song

Miss J. Hunter Dunn, Miss J. Hunter Dunn,
Furnish'd and burnish'd by Aldershot sun,
What strenuous singles we played after tea,
We in the tournament—you against me!

Love-thirty, love-forty, oh! weakness of joy,
The speed of a swallow, the grace of a boy,
With carefullest carelessness, gaily you won,
I am weak from your loveliness, Joan Hunter Dunn.

Miss Joan Hunter Dunn, Miss Joan Hunter Dunn,
How mad I am, sad I am, glad that you won.
The warm-handled racket is back in its press,
But my shock-headed victor, she loves me no less.

Her father's euonymus shines as we walk,
And swing past the summer-house, buried in talk,
And cool the verandah that welcomes us in
To the six-o'clock news and a lime-juice and gin.

The scent of the conifers, sound of the bath,
The view from my bedroom of moss-dappled path,
As I struggle with double-end evening tie,
For we dance at the Golf Club, my victor and I.

On the floor of her bedroom lie blazer and shorts
And the cream-coloured walls are be-trophied with sports,
And westering, questioning settles the sun
On your low-leaded window, Miss Joan Hunter Dunn.

The Hillman is waiting, the light's in the hall,
The pictures of Egypt are bright on the wall,
My sweet, I am standing beside the oak stair
And there on the landing's the light on your hair.

By roads 'not adopted', by woodlanded ways,
She drove to the club in the late summer haze,
Into nine-o'clock Camberley, heavy with bells
And mushroomy, pine-woody, evergreen smells.

Miss Joan Hunter Dunn, Miss Joan Hunter Dunn,
I can hear from the car-park the dance has begun.
Oh! full Surrey twilight! importunate band!
Oh! strongly adorable tennis-girl's hand!

Around us are Rovers and Austins afar,
Above us the intimate roof of the car,
And here on my right is the girl of my choice,
With the tilt of her nose and the chime of her voice,

And the scent of her wrap, and the words never said,
And the ominous, ominous dancing ahead.
We sat in the car park till twenty to one
And now I'm engaged to Miss Joan Hunter Dunn.

Indoor Games Near Newbury

In among the silver birches winding ways of tarmac wander
    And the signs to Bussock Bottom, Tussock Wood and Windy
                                        Brake,
Gabled lodges, tile-hung churches, catch the lights of our Lagonda
    As we drive to Wendy's party, lemon curd and Christmas cake.

        Rich the makes of motor whirring,
        Past the pine-plantation purring
            Come up, Hupmobile, Delage!
        Short the way your chauffeurs travel,
        Crunching over private gravel
            Each from out his warm garáge.

Oh but Wendy, when the carpet yielded to my indoor pumps
        There you stood, your gold hair streaming,
        Handsome in the hall-light gleaming
There you looked and there you led me off into the game of clumps
        Then the new Victrola playing
        And your funny uncle saying
'Choose your partners for a fox-trot! Dance until it's *tea* o'clock!
        'Come on, young 'uns, foot it featly!'
        Was it chance that paired us neatly,
        I who loved you so completely,
You who pressed me closely to you, hard against your party frock?

'Meet me when you've finished eating!' So we met and no one
                                        found us.
    Oh that dark and furry cupboard while the rest played hide and
                                        seek!
Holding hands our two hearts beating in the bedroom silence
                                        round us,
    Holding hands and hardly hearing sudden footstep, thud and
                                        shriek.
            Love that lay too deep for kissing—
            'Where *is* Wendy? Wendy's missing!'
                Love so pure it *had* to end,
            Love so strong that I was frighten'd
            When you gripped my fingers tight and
Hugging, whispered 'I'm your friend.'

Good-bye, Wendy! Send the fairies, pinewood elf and larch tree
                                        gnome,
            Spingle-spangled stars are peeping
            At the lush Lagonda creeping
Down the winding ways of tarmac to the leaded lights of home.
            There, among the silver birches,
            All the bells of all the churches
Sounded in the bath-waste running out into the frosty air.
            Wendy speeded my undressing,
            Wendy is the sheet's caressing
            Wendy bending gives a blessing,
Holds me as I drift to dreamland, safe inside my slumberwear.

Winter Seascape

The sea runs back against itself
    With scarcely time for breaking wave
To cannonade a slatey shelf
    And thunder under in a cave

Before the next can fully burst.
    The headwind, blowing harder still,
Smooths it to what it was at first—
    A slowly rolling water-hill.

Against the breeze the breakers haste,
    Against the tide their ridges run
And all the sea's a dappled waste
    Criss-crossing underneath the sun.

Far down the beach the ripples drag
    Blown backward, rearing from the shore,
And wailing gull and shrieking shag
    Alone can pierce the ocean roar.

Unheard, a mongrel hound gives tongue,
    Unheard are shouts of little boys:
What chance has any inland lung
    Against this multi-water noise?

Here where the cliffs alone prevail
    I stand exultant, neutral, free,
And from the cushion of the gale
    Behold a huge consoling sea.

Greenaway

I know so well this turfy mile,
    These clumps of sea-pink withered brown,
The breezy cliff, the awkward stile,
    The sandy path that takes me down

To crackling layers of broken slate
    Where black and flat sea-woodlice crawl
And isolated rock pools wait
    Wash from the highest tides of all.

I know the roughly blasted track
    That skirts a small and smelly bay
And over squelching bladderwrack
    Leads to the beach at Greenaway.

Down on the shingle safe at last
    I hear the slowly dragging roar
As mighty rollers mount to cast
    Small coal and seaweed on the shore,

And spurting far as it can reach
　　The shooting surf comes hissing round
To leave a line along the beach
　　Of cowries waiting to be found.

Tide after tide by night and day
　　The breakers battle with the land
And rounded smooth along the bay
　　The faithful rocks protecting stand.

But in a dream the other night
　　I saw this coastline from the sea
And felt the breakers plunging white
　　Their weight of waters over me.

There were the stile, the turf, the shore,
　　The safety line of shingle beach
With every stroke I struck the more
　　The backwash sucked me out of reach.

Back into what a water-world
　　Of waving weed and waiting claws?
Of writhing tentacles uncurled
　　To drag me to what dreadful jaws?

East Anglian Bathe

Oh when the early morning at the seaside
　　Took us with hurrying steps from Horsey Mere
To see the whistling bent-grass on the leeside
　　And then the tumbled breaker-line appear,
On high, the clouds with mighty adumbration
　　Sailed over us to seaward fast and clear
And jellyfish in quivering isolation
　　Lay silted in the dry sand of the breeze
And we, along the table-land of beach blown
　　Went gooseflesh from our shoulders to our knees
And ran to catch the football, each to each thrown,
　　In the soft and swirling music of the seas.

There splashed about our ankles as we waded
 Those intersecting wavelets morning-cold,
And sudden dark a patch of sea was shaded,
 And sudden light, another patch would hold
The warmth of whirling atoms in a sun-shot
 And underwater sandstorms green and gold.
So in we dived and louder than a gunshot
 Sea-water broke in fountains down the ear.
How cold the bathe, how chattering cold the drying,
 How welcoming the inland reeds appear,
The wood-smoke and the breakfast and the frying,
 And your warm freshwater ripples, Horsey Mere.

Sunday Morning, King's Cambridge

File into yellow candle light, fair choristers of King's
 Lost in the shadowy silence of canopied Renaissance stalls
In blazing glass above the dark glow skies and thrones and wings
 Blue, ruby, gold and green between the whiteness of the walls
And with what rich precision the stonework soars and springs
 To fountain out a spreading vault—a shower that never falls.

The white of windy Cambridge courts, the cobbles brown and dry,
 The gold of plaster Gothic with ivy overgrown,
The apple-red, the silver fronts, the wide green flats and high,
 The yellowing elm-trees circled out on islands of their own—
Oh, here behold all colours change that catch the flying sky
 To waves of pearly light that heave along the shafted stone.

In far East Anglian churches, the clasped hands lying long
 Recumbent on sepulchral slabs or effigied in brass
Buttress with prayer this vaulted roof so white and light and strong
 And countless congregations as the generations pass
Join choir and great crowned organ case, in centuries of song
 To praise Eternity contained in Time and coloured glass.

Bristol And Clifton

'Yes, I was only sidesman here when last
You came to Evening Communion.
But now I have retired from the bank
I have more leisure time for church finance.
We moved into a somewhat larger house
Than when you knew us in Manilla Road.
This is the window to my lady wife.
You cannot see it now, but in the day
The greens and golds are truly wonderful.'

'How very sad. I do not mean about
The window, but I mean about the death
Of Mrs. Battlecock. When did she die?'

'Two years ago when we had just moved in
To Pembroke Road. I rather fear the stairs
And basement kitchen were too much for her—
Not that, of course, she did the servants' work—
But supervising servants all the day
Meant quite a lot of climbing up and down.'
'How very sad. Poor Mrs. Battlecock.'
'"The glory that men do lives after them,"
And so I gave this window in her name.
It's executed by a Bristol firm;
The lady artist who designed it, made
The figure of the lady on the left
Something like Mrs. Battlecock.'
'How nice.'
                              'Yes, was it not? We had
A stained glass window on the stairs at home,
In Pembroke Road. But not so good as this.
This window is the glory of the church
At least I think so—and the unstained oak
Looks very chaste beneath it. When I gave
The oak, that brass inscription on your right
Commemorates the fact, the Dorcas Club
Made these blue kneelers, though we do not kneel:
We leave that to the Roman Catholics.'
'How very nice, indeed. How very nice.'

'Seeing I have some knowledge of finance
Our kind Parochial Church Council made
Me People's Warden, and I'm glad to say
That our collections are still keeping up.
The chancel has been flood lit, and the stove
Which used to heat the church was obsolete.
So now we've had some radiators fixed
Along the walls and eastward of the aisles;
This last I thought of lest at any time
A Ritualist should be inducted here
And want to put up altars. He would find
The radiators inconvenient.
Our only ritual here is with the Plate;
I think we make it dignified enough.
I take it up myself, and afterwards,
Count the Collection on the vestry safe.'

'Forgive me, aren't we talking rather loud?
I think I see a woman praying there.'
'Praying? The service is all over now
And here's the verger waiting to turn out
The lights and lock the church up. She cannot
Be Loyal Church of England. Well, good-bye.
Time flies. I must be going. Come again.
There are some pleasant people living here.
I know the Inskips very well indeed.'

The Village Inn

'The village inn, the dear old inn,
So ancient, clean and free from sin,
True centre of our rural life
Where Hodge sits down beside his wife
And talks of Marx and nuclear fission
With all a rustic's intuition.
Ah, more than church or school or hall,
The village inn's the heart of all.'
So spake the brewer's P.R.O.,
A man who really ought to know,
For he is paid for saying so.
And then he kindly gave to me
A lovely coloured booklet free.

'Twas full of prose that sang the praise
Of coaching inns in Georgian days,
Showing how public-houses are
More modern than the motor-car,
More English than the weald or wold
And almost equally as old,
And run for love and not for gold
Until I felt a filthy swine
For loathing beer and liking wine,
And rotten to the very core
For thinking village inns a bore,
And village bores more sure to roam
To village inns than stay at home.
And then I thought I *must* be wrong,
So up I rose and went along
To that old village alehouse where
In neon lights is written 'Bear',

Ah, where's the inn that once I knew
    With brick and chalky wall
Up which the knobbly pear-tree grew
    For fear the place would fall?

Oh, that old pot-house isn't there,
    It wasn't worth our while;
You'll find we have rebuilt 'The Bear'
    In Early Georgian style.

But winter jasmine used to cling
    With golden stars a-shine
Where rain and wind would wash and swing
    The crudely painted sign.

And where's the roof of golden thatch?
    The chimney-stack of stone?
The crown-glass panes that used to match
    Each sunset with their own?

Oh now the walls are red and smart,
    The roof has emerald tiles.
The neon sign's a work of art
    And visible for miles.

The bar inside was papered green,
   The settles grained like oak,
The only light was paraffin,
   The woodfire used to smoke.

And photographs from far and wide
   Were hung around the room:
The hunt, the church, the football side,
   And Kitchener of Khartoum.

Our air-conditioned bars are lined
   With washable material,
The stools are steel, the taste refined,
   Hygienic and ethereal.

Hurrah, hurrah, for hearts of oak!
   Away with inhibitions!
For here's a place to sit and soak
   In sanit'ry conditions.

Inexpensive Progress

Encase your legs in nylons,
Bestride your hills with pylons
   O age without a soul;
Away with gentle willows
And all the elmy billows
   That through your valleys roll.

Let's say good-bye to hedges
And roads with grassy edges
   And winding country lanes;
Let all things travel faster
Where motor-car is master
   Till only Speed remains.

Destroy the ancient inn-signs
But strew the roads with tin signs
   'Keep Left,' 'M4,' 'Keep Out!'
Command, instruction, warning,
Repetitive adorning
   The rockeried roundabout;

For every raw obscenity
Must have its small 'amenity,'
    Its patch of shaven green,
And hoardings look a wonder
In banks of floribunda
    With floodlights in between.

Leave no old village standing
Which could provide a landing
    For aeroplanes to roar,
But spare such cheap defacements
As huts with shuttered casements
    Unlived-in since the war.

Let no provincial High Street
Which might be your or my street
    Look as it used to do,
But let the chain stores place here
Their miles of black glass facia
    And traffic thunder through.

And if there is some scenery,
Some unpretentious greenery,
    Surviving anywhere,
It does not need protecting
For soon we'll be erecting
    A Power Station there.

When all our roads are lighted
By concrete monsters sited
    Like gallows overhead,
Bathed in the yellow vomit
Each monster belches from it,
    We'll know that we are dead.

Death In Leamington

She died in the upstairs bedroom
    By the light of the ev'ning star
That shone through the plate glass window
    From over Leamington Spa.

Beside her the lonely crochet
    Lay patiently and unstirred,
But the fingers that would have work'd it
    Were dead as the spoken word.

And Nurse came in with the tea-things
    Breast high 'mid the stands and chairs—
But Nurse was alone with her own little soul,
    And the things were alone with theirs.

She bolted the big round window,
    She let the blinds unroll,
She set a match to the mantle,
    She covered the fire with coal.

And 'Tea!' she said in a tiny voice
    'Wake up! It's nearly *five*.'
Oh! Chintzy, chintzy cheeriness,
    Half dead and half alive!

Do you know that the stucco is peeling?
    Do you know that the heart will stop?
From those yellow Italianate arches
    Do you hear the plaster drop?

Nurse looked at the silent bedstead,
    At the gray, decaying face,
As the calm of a Leamington ev'ning
    Drifted into the place.

She moved the table of bottles
    Away from the bed to the wall;
And tiptoeing gently over the stairs
    Turned down the gas in the hall.

On A Portrait Of A Deaf Man

The kind old face, the egg-shaped head,
    The tie, discreetly loud,
The loosely fitting shooting clothes,
    A closely fitting shroud.

91

He liked old City dining-rooms,
    Potatoes in their skin,
But now his mouth is wide to let
    The London clay come in.

He took me on long silent walks
    In country lanes when young,
He knew the name of ev'ry bird
    But not the song it sung.

And when he could not hear me speak
    He smiled and looked so wise
That now I do not like to think
    Of maggots in his eyes.

He liked the rain-washed Cornish air
    And smell of ploughed-up soil,
He liked a landscape big and bare
    And painted it in oil.

But least of all he liked that place
    Which hangs on Highgate Hill
Of soaked Carrara-covered earth
    For Londoners to fill.

He would have liked to say good-bye,
    Shake hands with many friends,
In Highgate now his finger-bones
    Stick through his finger-ends.

You, God, who treat him thus and thus,
    Say 'Save his soul and pray.'
You ask me to believe You and
    I only see decay.

A Child Ill

Oh, little body, do not die.
    The soul looks out through wide blue eyes
So questioningly into mine,
    That my tormented soul replies:

'Oh, little body, do not die.
    You hold the soul that talks to me
Although our conversation be
    As wordless as the windy sky.'

So looked my father at the last
    Right in my soul, before he died,
Though words we spoke went heedless past
    As London traffic-roar outside.

And now the same blue eyes I see
    Look through me from a little son,
So questioning, so searchingly
    That youthfulness and age are one.

My father looked at me and died
    Before my soul made full reply.
Lord, leave this other Light alight—
    Oh, little body, do not die.

Philip Larkin

Born Yesterday
for Sally Amis

Tightly-folded bud,
I have wished you something
None of the others would:
Not the usual stuff
About being beautiful,
Or running off a spring
Of innocence and love—
They will all wish you that,
And should it prove possible,
Well, you're a lucky girl.

But if it shouldn't, then
May you be ordinary;
Have, like other women,
An average of talents:
Not ugly, not good-looking,
Nothing uncustomary
To pull you off your balance,
That, unworkable itself,
Stops all the rest from working.
In fact, may you be dull—
If that is what a skilled,
Vigilant, flexible,
Unemphasized, enthralled
Catching of happiness is called.

Days

What are days for?
Days are where we live.
They come, they wake us
Time and time over.
They are to be happy in:
Where can we live but days?

Ah, solving that question
Brings the priest and the doctor
In their long coats
Running over the fields.

To The Sea

To step over the low wall that divides
Road from concrete walk above the shore
Brings sharply back something known long before—
The miniature gaiety of seasides.
Everything crowds under the low horizon:
Steep beach, blue water, towels, red bathing caps,
The small hushed waves' repeated fresh collapse
Up the warm yellow sand, and further off
A white steamer stuck in the afternoon—

Still going on, all of it, still going on!
To lie, eat, sleep in hearing of the surf
(Ears to transistors, that sound tame enough
Under the sky), or gently up and down
Lead the uncertain children, frilled in white
And grasping at enormous air, or wheel
The rigid old along for them to feel
A final summer, plainly still occurs
As half an annual pleasure, half a rite,

As when, happy at being on my own,
I searched the sand for Famous Cricketers,
Or, farther back, my parents, listeners
To the same seaside quack, first became known.
Strange to it now, I watch the cloudless scene:
The same clear water over smoothed pebbles,
The distant bathers' weak protesting trebles
Down at its edge, and then the cheap cigars,
The chocolate-papers, tea-leaves, and, between,

The rocks, the rusting soup-tins, till the first
Few families start the trek back to the cars.
The white steamer has gone. Like breathed-on glass
The sunlight has turned milky. If the worst
Of flawless weather is our falling short,
It may be that through habit these do best,
Coming to water clumsily undressed
Yearly; teaching their children by a sort
Of clowning; helping the old, too, as they ought.

The Whitsun Weddings

That Whitsun, I was late getting away:
    Not till about
One-twenty on the sunlit Saturday
Did my three-quarters-empty train pull out,
All windows down, all cushions hot, all sense
Of being in a hurry gone. We ran
Behind the backs of houses, crossed a street
Of blinding windscreens, smelt the fish-dock; thence
The river's level drifting breadth began,
Where sky and Lincolnshire and water meet.

All afternoon, through the tall heat that slept
    For miles inland,
A slow and stopping curve southwards we kept.
Wide farms went by, short-shadowed cattle, and
Canals with floatings of industrial froth;
A hothouse flashed uniquely: hedges dipped
And rose: and now and then a smell of grass
Displaced the reek of buttoned carriage-cloth
Until the next town, new and nondescript,
Approached with acres of dismantled cars.

At first, I didn't notice what a noise
    The weddings made
Each station that we stopped at: sun destroys
The interest of what's happening in the shade,
And down the long cool platforms whoops and skirls
I took for porters larking with the mails,
And went on reading. Once we started, though,
We passed them, grinning and pomaded, girls
In parodies of fashion, heels and veils,
All posed irresolutely, watching us go,

As if out on the end of an event
    Waving goodbye
To something that survived it. Struck, I leant
More promptly out next time, more curiously,
And saw it all again in different terms:
The fathers with broad belts under their suits
And seamy foreheads; mothers loud and fat;
An uncle shouting smut; and then the perms,
The nylon gloves and jewellery-substitutes,
The lemons, mauves, and olive-ochres that

Marked off the girls unreally from the rest.
    Yes, from cafés
And banquet-halls up yards, and bunting-dressed
Coach-party annexes, the wedding-days
Were coming to an end. All down the line
Fresh couples climbed aboard: the rest stood round;
The last confetti and advice were thrown,
And, as we moved, each face seemed to define
Just what it saw departing: children frowned
At something dull; fathers had never known

Success so huge and wholly farcical;
    The women shared
The secret like a happy funeral;
While girls, gripping their handbags tighter, stared
At a religious wounding. Free at last,
And loaded with the sum of all they saw,
We hurried towards London, shuffling gouts of steam.
Now fields were building-plots, and poplars cast
Long shadows over major roads, and for
Some fifty minutes, that in time would seem

98

Just long enough to settle hats and say
   I nearly died,
A dozen marriages got under way.
They watched the landscape, sitting side by side
—An Odeon went past, a cooling tower,
And someone running up to bowl—and none
Thought of the others they would never meet
Or how their lives would all contain this hour.
I thought of London spread out in the sun,
Its postal districts packed like squares of wheat:

There we were aimed. And as we raced across
   Bright knots of rail
Past standing Pullmans, walls of blackened moss
Came close, and it was nearly done, this frail
Travelling coincidence; and what it held
Stood ready to be loosed with all the power
That being changed can give. We slowed again,
And as the tightened brakes took hold, there swelled
A sense of falling, like an arrow-shower
Sent out of sight, somewhere becoming rain.

Mr Bleaney

'This was Mr Bleaney's room. He stayed
The whole time he was at the Bodies, till
They moved him.' Flowered curtains, thin and frayed,
Fall to within five inches of the sill,

Whose window shows a strip of building land,
Tussocky, littered. 'Mr Bleaney took
My bit of garden properly in hand.'
Bed, upright chair, sixty-watt bulb, no hook

Behind the door, no room for books or bags—
'I'll take it.' So it happens that I lie
Where Mr Bleaney lay, and stub my fags
On the same saucer-souvenir, and try

Stuffing my ears with cotton-wool, to drown
The jabbering set he egged her on to buy.
I know his habits—what time he came down,
His preference for sauce to gravy, why

He kept on plugging at the four aways—
Likewise their yearly frame: the Frinton folk
Who put him up for summer holidays,
And Christmas at his sister's house in Stoke.

But if he stood and watched the frigid wind
Tousling the clouds, lay on the fusty bed
Telling himself that this was home, and grinned,
And shivered, without shaking off the dread

That how we live measures our own nature,
And at his age having no more to show
Than one hired box should make him pretty sure
He warranted no better, I don't know.

Afternoons

Summer is fading:
The leaves fall in ones and twos
From trees bordering
The new recreation ground.
In the hollows of afternoons
Young mothers assemble
At swing and sandpit
Setting free their children.

Behind them, at intervals,
Stand husbands in skilled trades,
An estateful of washing,
And the albums, lettered
Our Wedding, lying
Near the television:
Before them, the wind
Is ruining their courting-places

That are still courting-places
(But the lovers are all in school),
And their children, so intent on
Finding more unripe acorns,
Expect to be taken home.
Their beauty has thickened.
Something is pushing them
To the side of their own lives.

Skin

Obedient daily dress,
You cannot always keep
That unfakable young surface.
You must learn your lines—
Anger, amusement, sleep;
Those few forbidding signs

Of the continuous coarse
Sand-laden wind, time;
You must thicken, work loose
Into an old bag
Carrying a soiled name.
Parch then; be roughened; sag;

And pardon me, that I
Could find, when you were new,
No brash festivity
To wear you at, such as
Clothes are entitled to
Till the fashion changes.

An Arundel Tomb

Side by side, their faces blurred,
The earl and countess lie in stone,
Their proper habits vaguely shown
As jointed armour, stiffened pleat,
And that faint hint of the absurd
The little dogs under their feet.

Such plainness of the pre-baroque
Hardly involves the eye, until
It meets his left-hand gauntlet, still
Clasped empty in the other; and
One sees, with a sharp tender shock,
His hand withdrawn, holding her hand.

They would not think to lie so long.
Such faithfulness in effigy
Was just a detail friends would see:
A sculptor's sweet commissioned grace
Thrown off in helping to prolong
The Latin names around the base.

They would not guess how early in
Their supine stationary voyage
The air would change to soundless damage,
Turn the old tenantry away;
How soon succeeding eyes begin
To look, not read. Rigidly they

Persisted, linked, through lengths and breadths
Of time. Snow fell, undated. Light
Each summer thronged the glass. A bright
Litter of birdcalls strewed the same
Bone-riddled ground. And up the paths
The endless altered people came,

Washing at their identity.
Now, helpless in the hollow of
An unarmorial age, a trough
Of smoke in slow suspended skeins
Above their scrap of history,
Only an attitude remains:

Time has transfigured them into
Untruth. The stone fidelity
They hardly meant has come to be
Their final blazon, and to prove
Our almost-instinct almost true:
What will survive of us is love.

The Building

Higher than the handsomest hotel
The lucent comb shows up for miles, but see,
All round it close-ribbed streets rise and fall
Like a great sigh out of the last century.
The porters are scruffy; what keep drawing up
At the entrance are not taxis; and in the hall
As well as creepers hangs a frightening smell.

There are paperbacks, and tea at so much a cup,
Like an airport lounge, but those who tamely sit
On rows of steel chairs turning the ripped mags
Haven't come far. More like a local bus,
These outdoor clothes and half-filled shopping bags
And faces restless and resigned, although
Every few minutes comes a kind of nurse

To fetch someone away: the rest refit
Cups back to saucers, cough, or glance below
Seats for dropped gloves or cards. Humans, caught
On ground curiously neutral, homes and names
Suddenly in abeyance; some are young,
Some old, but most at that vague age that claims
The end of choice, the last of hope; and all

Here to confess that something has gone wrong.
It must be error of a serious sort,
For see how many floors it needs, how tall
It's grown by now, and how much money goes
In trying to correct it. See the time,
Half-past eleven on a working day,
And these picked out of it; see, as they climb

To their appointed levels, how their eyes
Go to each other, guessing; on the way
Someone's wheeled past, in washed-to-rags ward clothes:
They see him, too. They're quiet. To realise
This new thing held in common makes them quiet,
For past these doors are rooms, and rooms past those,
And more rooms yet, each one further off

And harder to return from; and who knows
Which he will see, and when? For the moment, wait,
Look down at the yard. Outside seems old enough:
Red brick, lagged pipes, and someone walking by it
Out to the car park, free. Then, past the gate,
Traffic; a locked church; short terraced streets
Where kids chalk games, and girls with hair-dos fetch

Their separates from the cleaners—O world,
Your loves, your chances, are beyond the stretch
Of any hand from here! And so, unreal,
A touching dream to which we all are lulled
But wake from separately. In it, conceits
And self-protecting ignorance congeal
To carry life, collapsing only when

Called to these corridors (for now once more
The nurse beckons—). Each gets up and goes
At last. Some will be out by lunch, or four;
Others, not knowing it, have come to join
The unseen congregations whose white rows
Lie set apart above—women, men;
Old, young; crude facets of the only coin

This place accepts. All know they are going to die.
Not yet, perhaps, not here, but in the end,
And somewhere like this. That is what it means,
This clean-sliced cliff; a struggle to transcend
The thought of dying, for unless its powers
Outbuild cathedrals nothing contravenes
The coming dark, though crowds each evening try

With wasteful, weak, propitiatory flowers.

Going, Going

I thought it would last my time—
The sense that, beyond the town,
There would always be fields and farms,
Where the village louts could climb
Such trees as were not cut down;
I knew there'd be false alarms

In the papers about old streets
And split-level shopping, but some
Have always been left so far;
And when the old part retreats
As the bleak high-risers come
We can always escape in the car.

Things are tougher than we are, just
As earth will always respond
However we mess it about;
Chuck filth in the sea, if you must:
The tides will be clean beyond.
—But what do I feel now? Doubt?

Or age, simply? The crowd
Is young in the M1 cafe;
Their kids are screaming for more—
More houses, more parking allowed,
More caravan sites, more pay.
On the Business Page, a score

Of spectacled grins approve
Some takeover bid that entails
Five per cent profit (and ten
Per cent more in the estuaries): move
Your works to the unspoilt dales
(Grey area grants)! And when

You try to get near the sea
In summer . . .
                    It seems, just now,
To be happening so very fast;
Despite all the land left free
For the first time I feel somehow
That it isn't going to last,

That before I snuff it, the whole
Boiling will be bricked in
Except for the tourist parts—
First slum of Europe: a role
It won't be so hard to win,
With a cast of crooks and tarts.

And that will be England gone,
The shadows, the meadows, the lanes,
The guildhalls, the carved choirs,
There'll be books; it will linger on
In galleries; but all that remains
For us will be concrete and trees.

Most things are never meant.
This won't be, most likely; but greeds
And garbage are too thick-strewn
To be swept up now, or invent
Excuses that make them all needs.
I just think it will happen, soon.

The Trees

The trees are coming into leaf
Like something almost being said;
The recent buds relax and spread,
Their greenness is a kind of grief.

Is it that they are born again
And we grow old? No, they die too.
Their yearly trick of looking new
Is written down in rings of grain.

Yet still the unresting castles thresh
In fullgrown thickness every May.
Last year is dead, they seem to say,
Begin afresh, afresh, afresh.

The Explosion

On the day of the explosion
Shadows pointed towards the pithead:
In the sun the slagheap slept.

Down the lane came men in pitboots
Coughing oath-edged talk and pipe-smoke
Shouldering off the freshened silence.

One chased after rabbits: lost them;
Came back with a nest of lark's eggs;
Showed them; lodged them in the grasses.

So they passed in beards and moleskins,
Fathers, brothers, nicknames, laughter,
Through the tall gates standing open.

At noon, there came a tremor; cows
Stopped chewing for a second; sun,
Scarfed as in a heat-haze, dimmed.

The dead go on before us, they
Are sitting in God's house in comfort,
We shall see them face to face—

Plain as lettering in the chapels
It was said, and for a second
Wives saw men of the explosion

Larger than in life they managed—
Gold as on a coin, or walking
Somehow from the sun towards them,

One showing the eggs unbroken.

R. S. Thomas

Song

We, who are men, how shall we know
Earth's ecstasy, who feels the plough
Probing her womb,
And after, the sweet gestation
And the year's care for her condition?
We, who have forgotten, so long ago
It happened, our own orgasm,
When the wind mixed with our limbs
And the sun had suck at our bosom;
We, who have affected the livery
Of the times' prudery,
How shall we quicken again
To the lust and thrust of the sun
And the seedling rain?

Soil

A field with tall hedges and a young
Moon in the branches and one star
Declining westward set the scene
Where he works slowly astride the rows
Of red mangolds and green swedes
Plying mechanically his cold blade.

This is his world, the hedge defines
The mind's limits; only the sky
Is boundless, and he never looks up;
His gaze is deep in the dark soil,
As are his feet. The soil is all;
His hands fondle it, and his bones
Are formed out of it with the swedes.
And if sometimes the knife errs,
Burying itself in his shocked flesh,
Then out of the wound the blood seeps home
To the warm soil from which it came.

Welsh Landscape

To live in Wales is to be conscious
At dusk of the spilled blood
That went to the making of the wild sky,
Dyeing the immaculate rivers
In all their courses.
It is to be aware,
Above the noisy tractor
And hum of the machine
Of strife in the strung woods,
Vibrant with sped arrows.
You cannot live in the present,
At least not in Wales.
There is the language for instance,
The soft consonants
Strange to the ear.
There are cries in the dark at night
As owls answer the moon,
And thick ambush of shadows,
Hushed at the fields' corners.
There is no present in Wales,
And no future;
There is only the past,
Brittle with relics,
Wind-bitten towers and castles
With sham ghosts;
Mouldering quarries and mines;
And an impotent people,
Sick with inbreeding,
Worrying the carcase of an old song.

Depopulation Of The Hills

Leave it, leave it—the hole under the door
Was a mouth through which the rough wind spoke
Ever more sharply; the dank hand
Of age was busy on the walls
Scrawling in blurred characters
Messages of hate and fear.

Leave it, leave it—the cold rain began
At summer end—there is no road
Over the bog, and winter comes
With mud above the axletree.

Leave it, leave it—the rain dripped
Day and night from the patched roof
Sagging beneath its load of sky.

Did the earth help them, time befriend
These last survivors? Did the spring grass
Heal winter's ravages? The grass
Wrecked them in its draughty tides,
Grew from the chimney-stack like smoke,
Burned its way through the weak timbers.
That was nature's jest, the sides
Of the old hulk cracked, but not with mirth.

The Village

Scarcely a street, too few houses
To merit the title; just a way between
The one tavern and the one shop
That leads nowhere and fails at the top
Of the short hill, eaten away
By long erosion of the green tide
Of grass creeping perpetually nearer
This last outpost of time past.

So little happens; the black dog
Cracking his fleas in the hot sun
Is history. Yet the girl who crosses
From door to door moves to a scale
Beyond the bland day's two dimensions.

Stay, then, village, for round you spins
On slow axis a world as vast
And meaningful as any poised
By great Plato's solitary mind.

Affinity

Consider this man in the field beneath,
Gaitered with mud, lost in his own breath,
Without joy, without sorrow,
Without children, without wife,
Stumbling insensitively from furrow to furrow,
A vague somnambulist; but hold your tears,
For his name also is written in the Book of Life.

Ransack your brainbox, pull out the drawers
That rot in your heart's dust, and what have you to give
To enrich his spirit or the way he lives?
From the standpoint of education or caste or creed
Is there anything to show that your essential need
Is less than his, who has the world for church,
And stands bare-headed in the woods' wide porch
Morning and evening to hear God's choir
Scatter their praises? Don't be taken in
By stinking garments or an aimless grin;
He also is human, and the same small star,
That lights you homeward, has inflamed his mind
With the old hunger, born of his kind.

The Last Of The Peasantry

What does he know? moving through the fields
And the wood's echoing cloisters
With a beast's gait, hunger in his eyes
Only for what the flat earth supplies;
His wisdom dwindled to a small gift
For handling stock, planting a few seeds
To ripen slowly in the warm breath
Of an old God to whom he never prays.

Moving through the fields, or still at home,
Dwarfed by its shadow on the bright wall,
His face is lit always from without,
The sun by day, the red fire at night;
Within is dark and bare, the grey ash
Is cold now, blow on it as you will.

The Poacher

Turning aside, never meeting
In the still lanes, fly infested,
Our frank greeting with quick smile,
You are the wind that set the bramble
Aimlessly clawing the void air.
The fox knows you, the sly weasel
Feels always the steel comb
Of eyes parting like sharp rain
Among the grasses its smooth fur.
No smoke haunting the cold chimney
Over your hearth betrays your dwelling
In blue writing above the trees.
The robed night, your familiar,
Covers your movements; the slick sun,
A dawn accomplice, removes your tracks
One by one from the bright dew.

The Lonely Farmer

Poor hill farmer astray in the grass:
There came a movement and he looked up, but
All that he saw was the wind pass.
There was a sound of voices on the air,
But where, where? It was only the glib stream talking
Softly to itself. And once when he was walking
Along a lane in spring he was deceived
By a shrill whistle coming through the leaves:
Wait a minute, wait a minute—four swift notes;
He turned, and it was nothing, only a thrush
In the thorn bushes easing its throat.
He swore at himself for paying heed,
The poor hill farmer, so often again
Stopping, staring, listening, in vain,
His ear betrayed by the heart's need.

A Peasant

Iago Prytherch his name, though, be it allowed,
Just an ordinary man of the bald Welsh hills,
Who pens a few sheep in a gap of cloud.
Docking mangels, chipping the green skin
From the yellow bones with a half-witted grin
Of satisfaction, or churning the crude earth
To a stiff sea of clods that glint in the wind—
So are his days spent, his spittled mirth
Rarer than the sun that cracks the cheeks
Of the gaunt sky perhaps once in a week.
And then at night see him fixed in his chair
Motionless, except when he leans to gob in the fire.
There is something frightening in the vacancy of his mind.
His clothes, sour with years of sweat
And animal contact, shock the refined,
But affected, sense with their stark naturalness.
Yet this is your prototype, who, season by season
Against siege of rain and the wind's attrition,
Preserves his stock, an impregnable fortress
Not to be stormed even in death's confusion.
Remember him, then, for he, too, is a winner of wars,
Enduring like a tree under the curious stars.

Invasion On The Farm

I am Prytherch. Forgive me. I don't know
What you are talking about; your thoughts flow
Too swiftly for me; I cannot dawdle
Along their banks and fish in their quick stream
With crude fingers. I am alone, exposed
In my own fields with no place to run
From your sharp eyes. I, who a moment back
Paddled in the bright grass, the old farm
Warm as a sack about me, feel the cold
Winds of the world blowing. The patched gate
You left open will never be shut again.

Cynddylan On A Tractor

Ah, you should see Cynddylan on a tractor.
Gone the old look that yoked him to the soil;
He's a new man now, part of the machine,
His nerves of metal and his blood oil.
The clutch curses, but the gears obey
His least bidding, and lo, he's away
Out of the farmyard, scattering hens.
Riding to work now as a great man should,
He is the knight at arms breaking the fields'
Mirror of silence, emptying the wood
Of foxes and squirrels and bright jays.
The sun comes over the tall trees
Kindling all the hedges, but not for him
Who runs his engine on a different fuel.
And all the birds are singing, bills wide in vain,
As Cynddylan passes proudly up the lane.

Death Of A Peasant

You remember Davies? He died, you know,
With his face to the wall, as the manner is
Of the poor peasant in his stone croft
On the Welsh hills. I recall the room
Under the slates, and the smirched snow
Of the wide bed in which he lay,
Lonely as an ewe that is sick to lamb
In the hard weather of mid-March.
I remember also the trapped wind
Tearing the curtains, and the wild light's
Frequent hysteria upon the floor,
The bare floor without a rug
Or mat to soften the loud tread
Of neighbours crossing the uneasy boards
To peer at Davies with gruff words
Of meaningless comfort, before they turned
Heartless away from the stale smell
Of death in league with those dank walls.

The Evacuee

She woke up under a loose quilt
Of leaf patterns, woven by the light
At the small window, busy with the boughs
Of a young cherry; but wearily she lay,
Waiting for the siren, slow to trust
Nature's deceptive peace, and then afraid
Of the long silence, she would have crept
Uneasily from the bedroom with its frieze
Of fresh sunlight, had not a cock crowed,
Shattering the surface of that limpid pool
Of stillness, and before the ripples died
One by one in the field's shallows,
The farm woke with uninhibited din.

And now the noise and not the silence drew her
Down the bare stairs at great speed.
The sounds and voices were a rough sheet
Waiting to catch her, as though she leaped
From a scorched storey of the charred past.

And there the table and the gallery
Of farm faces trying to be kind
Beckoned her nearer, and she sat down
Under the awning of salt hams.

And so she grew, a small bird in the nest
Of welcome that was built about her,
Home now after so long away
In the flowerless streets of the drab town.
The men watched her busy with the hens,
The soft flesh ripening warm as corn
On the sticks of limbs, the grey eyes clear,
Rinsed with dew of their long dread.
The men watched her, and, nodding, smiled
With earth's charity, patient and strong.

Laurie Lee

Thistle

Thistle, blue bunch of daggers
rattling upon the wind,
saw-tooth that separates
the lips of grasses.

Your wound in childhood was
a savage shock of joy
that set the bees on fire
and the loud larks singing.

Your head enchanted then
smouldering among the flowers
filled the whole sky with smoke
and sparks of seed.

Now from your stabbing bloom's
nostalgic point of pain
ghosts of those summers rise
rustling across my eyes.

Seeding a magic thorn
to prick the memory,
to start in my icy flesh
fevers of long lost fields.

First Love

That was her beginning, an apparition
of rose in the unbreathed airs of his love,
her heart revealed by the wash of summer
sprung from her childhood's shallow stream.

Then it was that she put up her hair,
inscribed her eyes with a look of grief,
while her limbs grew as curious as coral branches,
her breast full of secrets.

But the boy, confused in his day's desire,
was searching for herons, his fingers bathed
in the green of walnuts, or watching at night
the Great Bear spin from the maypole star.

It was then that he paused in the death of a game,
felt the hook of her hair on his swimming throat,
saw her mouth at large in the dark river
flushed like a salmon.

But he covered his face and hid his joy
in a wild-goose web of false directions,
and hunted the woods for eggs and glow-worms,
for rabbits tasteless as moss.

And she walked in fields where the crocuses
branded her feet, and mares' tails sprang
from the prancing lake, and the salty grasses
surged round her stranded body.

Milkmaid

The girl's faint treble, muted to the heat,
calls like a fainting bird across the fields
to where her flock lies panting for her voice,
their black horns buried deep in marigolds.

They climb awake, like drowsy butterflies,
and press their red flanks through the tall branched grass,
and as they go their wandering tongues embrace
the vacant summer mirrored in their eyes.

Led to the limestone shadows of a barn
they snuff their past embalmèd in the hay,
while her cool hand, cupped to the udder's fount,
distils the brimming harvest of their day.

Look, what a cloudy cream the earth gives out,
fat juice of buttercups and meadow-rye;
the girl dreams milk within her body's field
and hears, far off, her muted children cry.

April Rise

If ever I saw blessing in the air
    I see it now in this still early day
Where lemon-green the vaporous morning drips
    Wet sunlight on the powder of my eye.

Blown bubble-film of blue, the sky wraps round
    Weeds of warm light whose every root and rod
Splutters with soapy green, and all the world
    Sweats with the bead of summer in its bud.

If ever I heard blessing it is there
    Where birds in trees that shoals and shadows are
Splash with their hidden wings and drops of sound
    Break on my ears their crests of throbbing air.

Pure in the haze the emerald sun dilates,
    The lips of sparrows milk the mossy stones,
While white as water by the lake a girl
    Swims her green hand among the gathered swans.

Now, as the almond burns its smoking wick,
    Dropping small flames to light the candled grass;
Now, as my low blood scales its second chance,
    If ever world were blessèd, now it is.

Day Of These Days

Such a morning it is when love
leans through geranium windows
and calls with a cockerel's tongue.

When red-haired girls scamper like roses
over the rain-green grass,
and the sun drips honey.

When hedgerows grow venerable,
berries dry black as blood,
and holes suck in their bees.

Such a morning it is when mice
run whispering from the church,
dragging dropped ears of harvest.

When the partridge draws back his spring
and shoots like a buzzing arrow
over grained and mahogany fields.

When no table is bare,
and no breast dry,
and the tramp feeds off ribs of rabbit.

Such a day it is when time
piles up the hills like pumpkins,
and the streams run golden.

When all men smell good,
and the cheeks of girls
are as baked bread to the mouth.

As bread and beanflowers
the touch of their lips,
and their white teeth sweeter than cucumbers.

Apples

Behold the apples' rounded worlds:
juice-green of July rain,
the black polestar of flower, the rind
mapped with its crimson stain.

The russet, crab and cottage red
burn to the sun's hot brass,
then drop like sweat from every branch
and bubble in the grass.

They lie as wanton as they fall,
and where they fall and break,
the stallion clamps his crunching jaws,
the starling stabs his beak.

In each plump gourd the cidery bite
of boys' teeth tears the skin;
the waltzing wasp consumes his share,
the bent worm enters in.

I, with as easy hunger, take
entire my season's dole;
welcome the ripe, the sweet, the sour,
the hollow and the whole.

Cock Pheasant

Gilded with leaf-thick paint; a steady
Eye fixed like a ruby rock;
Across the cidrous banks of autumn
Swaggers the stamping pheasant-cock.

The thrusting nut and bursting apple
Accompany his jointed walk,
The creviced pumpkin and the marrow
Bend to his path on melting stalk.

Sure as an Inca priest or devil,
Feathers stroking down the corn,
He blinks the lively dust of daylight,
Blind to the hunter's powder-horn.

For me, alike, this flushed October—
Ripe, and round-fleshed, and bellyful—
Fevers me fast but cannot fright, though
Each dropped leaf shows the winter's skull.

Town Owl

On eves of cold, when slow coal fires,
rooted in basements, burn and branch,
brushing with smoke the city air;

When quartered moons pale in the sky,
and neons glow along the dark
likely deadly nightshade on a briar;

Above the muffled traffic then
I hear the owl, and at his note
I shudder in my private chair.

For like an augur he has come
to roost among our crumbling walls,
his blooded talons sheathed in fur.

Some secret lure of time it seems
has called him from his country wastes
to hunt a newer wasteland here.

And where the candelabra swung
bright with the dancers' thousand eyes,
now his black, hooded pupils stare,

And where the silk-shoed lovers ran
with dust of diamonds in their hair,
he opens now his silent wing,

And, like a stroke of doom, drops down,
and swoops across the empty hall,
and plucks a quick mouse off the stair . . .

Sunken Evening

The green light floods the city square—
   A sea of fowl and feathered fish,
   Where squalls of rainbirds dive and splash
And gusty sparrows chop the air.

Submerged, the prawn-blue pigeons feed
   In sandy grottoes round the Mall,
   And crusted lobster-buses crawl
Among the fountains' silver weed.

There, like a wreck, with mast and bell,
   The torn church settles by the bow,
   While phosphorescent starlings stow
Their mussel shells along the hull.

The oyster-poet, drowned but dry,
   Rolls a black pearl between his bones;
   The typist, trapped by telephones,
Gazes in bubbles at the sky.

Till, with the dark, the shallows run,
   And homeward surges tide and fret—
   The slow night trawls its heavy net
And hauls the clerk to Surbiton.

Field Of Autumn

Slow moves the acid breath of noon
over the copper-coated hill,
slow from the wild crab's bearded breast
the palsied apples fall.

Like coloured smoke the day hangs fire,
taking the village without sound;
the vulture-headed sun lies low
chained to the violet ground.

The horse upon the rocky height
rolls all the valley in his eye,
but dares not raise his foot or move
his shoulder from the fly.

The sheep, snail-backed against the wall,
lifts her blind face but does not know
the cry her blackened tongue gives forth
is the first bleat of snow.

Each bird and stone, each roof and well,
feels the gold foot of autumn pass;
each spider binds with glittering snare
the splintered bones of grass.

Slow moves the hour that sucks our life,
slow drops the late wasp from the pear,
the rose tree's thread of scent draws thin—
and snaps upon the air.

Christmas Landscape

Tonight the wind gnaws
with teeth of glass,
the jackdaw shivers
in caged branches of iron,
the stars have talons.

There is hunger in the mouth
of vole and badger,
silver agonies of breath
in the nostril of the fox,
ice on the rabbit's paw.

Tonight has no moon,
no food for the pilgrim;
the fruit tree is bare,
the rose bush a thorn
and the ground is bitter with stones.

But the mole sleeps, and the hedgehog
lies curled in a womb of leaves,
the bean and the wheat-seed
hug their germs in the earth
and the stream moves under the ice.

Tonight there is no moon,
but a new star opens
like a silver trumpet over the dead.
Tonight in a nest of ruins
the blessèd babe is laid.

And the fir tree warms to a bloom of candles,
the child lights his lantern,
stares at his tinselled toy;
our hearts and hearths
smoulder with live ashes.

In the blood of our grief
the cold earth is suckled,
in our agony the womb
convulses its seed,
in the cry of anguish
the child's first breath is born.

The Long War

Less passionate the long war throws
its burning thorn about all men,
caught in one grief, we share one wound,
and cry one dialect of pain.

We have forgot who fired the house,
whose easy mischief spilt first blood,
under one raging roof we lie
the fault no longer understood.

But as our twisted arms embrace
the desert where our cities stood,
death's family likeness in each face
must show, at last, our brotherhood.

Charles Causley

The Seasons In North Cornwall

O spring has set off her green fuses
    Down by the Tamar today,
And careless, like tide-marks, the hedges
    Are bursting with almond and may.

Here lie I, waiting for old summer,
    A red face and straw-coloured hair has he:
I shall meet him on the road from Marazion
    And the Mediterranean Sea.

September has flung a spray of rooks
    On the sea-chart of the sky,
The tall shipmasts crack in the forest
    And the banners of autumn fly.

My room is a bright glass cabin,
    All Cornwall thunders at my door,
And the white ships of winter lie
    In the sea-roads of the moor.

Mary, Mary Magdalene

On the east wall of the church of St Mary Magdalene at
Launceston in Cornwall is a granite figure of the saint. The
children of the town say that a stone lodged on her back will bring
good luck.

Mary, Mary Magdalene
Lying on the wall,
I throw a pebble on your back.
Will it lie or fall?

Send me down for Christmas
Some stockings and some hose,
And send before the winter's end
A brand-new suit of clothes.

Mary, Mary Magdalene
Under a stony tree,
I throw a pebble on your back.
What will you send me?

I'll send you for your christening
A woollen robe to wear,
A shiny cup from which to sup,
And a name to bear.

Mary, Mary Magdalene
Lying cool as snow,
What will you be sending me
When to school I go?

I'll send a pencil and a pen
That write both clean and neat,
And I'll send to the schoolmaster
A tongue that's kind and sweet.

Mary, Mary Magdalene
Lying in the sun,
What will you be sending me
Now I'm twenty-one?

I'll send you down a locket
As silver as your skin,
And I'll send you a lover
To fit a gold key in.

Mary, Mary Magdalene
Underneath the spray,
What will you be sending me
On my wedding-day?

I'll send you down some blossom,
Some ribbons and some lace,
And for the bride a veil to hide
The blushes on her face.

Mary, Mary Magdalene
Whiter than the swan,
Tell me what you'll send me,
Now my good man's dead and gone.

I'll send to you a single bed
On which you must lie,
And pillows bright where tears may light
That fall from your eye.

Mary, Mary Magdalene
Now nine months are done,
What will you be sending me
For my little son?

I'll send you for your baby
A lucky stone, and small,
To throw to Mary Magdalene
Lying on the wall.

By St Thomas Water

By St Thomas Water
Where the river is thin
We looked for a jam-jar
To catch the quick fish in.
Through St Thomas Churchyard
Jessie and I ran
The day we took the jam-pot
Off the dead man.

On the scuffed tombstone
The grey flowers fell,
Cracked was the water,
Silent the shell.
The snake for an emblem
Swirled on the slab,
Across the beach of sky the sun
Crawled like a crab.

'If we walk,' said Jessie,
'Seven times round,
We shall hear a dead man
Speaking underground.'
Round the stone we danced, we sang,
Watched the sun drop,
Laid our heads and listened
At the tomb-top.

Soft as the thunder
At the storm's start
I heard a voice as clear as blood,
Strong as the heart.
But what words were spoken
I can never say,
I shut my fingers round my head,
Drove them away.

'What are those letters, Jessie,
Cut so sharp and trim
All round this holy stone
With earth up to the brim?'
Jessie traced the letters
Black as coffin-lead.
'He is not dead but sleeping,'
Slowly she said.

I looked at Jessie,
Jessie looked at me,
And our eyes in wonder
Grew wide as the sea.
Past the green and bending stones
We fled hand in hand,
Silent through the tongues of grass
To the river strand.

By the creaking cypress
We moved as soft as smoke
For fear all the people
Underneath awoke.
Over all the sleepers
We darted light as snow
In case they opened up their eyes,
Called us from below.

Many a day has faltered
Into many a year
Since the dead awoke and spoke
And we would not hear.
Waiting in the cold grass
Under a crinkled bough,
Quiet stone, cautious stone,
What do you tell me now?

Reservoir Street

In nineteen twenty-six, the year
Of the Strike, on a day of bubbling heat
I went to stay with my sun-faced cousins
Who lived in a house on Reservoir Street.

Auntie stood strong as the Eddystone Lighthouse.
A terrible light shone out of her head.
Her children scuttled like ships for harbour.
'You must let them know what's what,' she said.

Her five prime-beef boys circled round me.
They didn't enjoy what they saw at all.
We couldn't make any more of each other
Than the map of stains on the bedroom wall.

All night long on the road to the city
The motor-car tyres rubbed out the dark.
Early in the morning I watched from the window
The sun like a killer come out of the park.

Down in the reservoir I saw a man drowning.
His flooding head came over the side.
They poked him out of a parcel of water.
'He's poisoned the drink!' my cousins cried.

I packed my bag and I said to Auntie,
'I think I'll go home on the one o'clock train.'
'My,' they all said, 'he wants his mammy.'
They never let me forget it again.

Through the Cornish jungle-country
Like a parrot the train screamed home.
I thought of my brother who slept beside me,
Four walls round us pure as cloam.

When I got to the house my head was thunder.
The bed lay open as a shell.
Sweet was my brother's kiss, and sweeter
The innocent water from the well.

Dockacre

Two doors away, at Dockacre, a ghost
In an isosceles cap assembles just before dawn,
Jerks round the ripped garden, through the dog-gates
And up the buckled stairs, quietly playing a flute.

Often, sleepless in a bland electric glare
(Since I slept on the mess-deck, to wake up
Without a pilot-light gives me the feeling
I'm going to be drowned) I've tried to hear it

Rounding the hollyhocks for the front door, but so far
It's always been the paper-train. The ghost's name
Is Nicholas Herle, once High Sheriff of Cornwall.
On the wall at Dockacre there's a creamy portrait of the wife

Who was shot by accident, stabbed, or driven mad,
No-one seems quite certain which, though probably
It was the last. In a curled account
He shut the girl in a dark room, trying

To starve her to sanity. She died of the cure
On Christmas Day, 1714, and Nicholas left for Hampstead,
But we've never forgotten her, or him.
My neighbour still has the bald flute. It's part

Of a cane walking-stick. He kindly offered
To play it to me once, but I declined,
Fearing that I might hear it again in the chopped hours:
Nicholas playing his inaccurate, sad tunes

As I whistled mine; both of us suffering from the same
Malaise that evidently even death won't cure.
I feared that as I looked towards my bedroom door
I should see the handle break slowly into flames, then turn.

Nursery Rhyme Of Innocence And Experience

I had a silver penny
   And an apricot tree
And I said to the sailor
   On the white quay

'Sailor O sailor
   Will you bring me
If I give you my penny
   And my apricot tree

'A fez from Algeria
   An Arab drum to beat
A little gilt sword
   And a parakeet?'

And he smiled and he kissed me
   As strong as death
And I saw his red tongue
   And I felt his sweet breath

'You may keep your penny
   And your apricot tree
And I'll bring your presents
   Back from sea.'

O the ship dipped down
    On the rim of the sky
And I waited while three
    Long summers went by

Then one steel morning
    On the white quay
I saw a grey ship
    Come in from sea

Slowly she came
    Across the bay
For her flashing rigging
    Was shot away

All round her wake
    The seabirds cried
And flew in and out
    Of the hole in her side

Slowly she came
    In the path of the sun
And I heard the sound
    Of a distant gun

And a stranger came running
    Up to me
From the deck of the ship
    And he said, said he

'O are you the boy
    Who would wait on the quay
With the silver penny
    And the apricot tree?

'I've a plum-coloured fez
    And a drum for thee
And a sword and a parakeet
    From over the sea.'

'O where is the sailor
    With bold red hair?
And what is that volley
    On the bright air?

'O where are the other
    Girls and boys?
And why have you brought me
    Children's toys?'

John Polruddon

John Polruddon
All of a sudden
Went out of his house one night,

    When a privateer
    Came sailing near
    Under his window-light.

They saw his jugs
His plates and mugs
His hearth as bright as brass,

    His gews and gaws
    And kicks and shaws
    All through his spying-glass.

They saw his wine
His silver shine
They heard his fiddlers play.

    'Tonight,' they said,
    'Out of his bed
    Polruddon we'll take away.'

And from a skiff
They climbed the cliff
And crossed the salt-wet lawn,

And as they crept
Polruddon slept
The night away to dawn.

'In air or ground
What is that sound?'
Polruddon said, and stirred.

They breathed, 'Be still,
It was the shrill
Of the scritch-owl you heard.'

'O yet again
I hear it plain,
But do I wake or dream?

'In morning's fog
The otter-dog
Is whistling by the stream.

'Now from the sea
What comes for me
Beneath my window dark?'

'Lie still, my dear,
All that you hear
Is the red fox's bark.'

Swift from his bed
Polruddon was sped
Before the day was white,

And head and feet
Wrapped in a sheet
They bore him down the height.

And never more
Through his own door
Polruddon went nor came,

Though many a tide
Has turned beside
The cliff that bears his name.

On stone and brick
Was ivy thick,
And the grey roof was thin,

And winter's gale
With fists of hail
Broke all the windows in.

The chimney-crown
Is tumbled down
And up grew the green,

Till on the cliff
It was as if
A house had never been.

But when the moon
Swims late or soon
Across St Austell Bay,

What sight, what sound
Haunts air and ground
Where once Polruddon lay?

It is the high
White scritch-owl's cry,
The fox as dark as blood,

And on the hill
The otter still
Whistles beside the flood.

Innocent's Song

Who's that knocking on the window,
Who's that standing at the door,
What are all those presents
Lying on the kitchen floor?

Who is the smiling stranger
With hair as white as gin,
What is he doing with the children
And who could have let him in?

Why has he rubies on his fingers,
A cold, cold crown on his head,
Why, when he caws his carol,
Does the salty snow run red?'

Why does he ferry my fireside
As a spider on a thread,
His fingers made of fuses
And his tongue of gingerbread?

Why does the world before him
Melt in a million suns,
Why doe his yellow, yearning eyes
Burn like saffron buns?

Watch where he comes walking
Out of the Christmas flame,
Dancing, double-talking:

Herod is his name.

The Ballad Of Charlotte Dymond

Charlotte Dymond, a domestic servant aged eighteen, was
murdered near Rowtor Ford on Bodmin Moor on Sunday, 14
April 1844, by her young man, a crippled farm-hand, Matthew
Weeks, aged twenty-two. A stone marks the spot.

It was a Sunday evening
    And in the April rain
That Charlotte went from our house
    And never came home again.

Her shawl of diamond redcloth,
    She wore a yellow gown,
She carried the green gauze handkerchief
    She bought in Bodmin town.

About her throat her necklace
    And in her purse her pay:
The four silver shillings
    She had at Lady Day.

In her purse four shillings
    And in her purse her pride
As she walked out one evening
    Her lover at her side.

Out beyond the marshes
    Where the cattle stand,
With her crippled lover
    Limping at her hand.

Charlotte walked with Matthew
    Through the Sunday mist,
Never saw the razor
    Waiting at his wrist.

Charlotte she was gentle
    But they found her in the flood
Her Sunday beads among the reeds
    Beaming with her blood.

Matthew, where is Charlotte,
    And wherefore has she flown?
For you walked out together
    And now are come alone.

Why do you not answer,
    Stand silent as a tree,
Your Sunday worsted stockings
    All muddied to the knee?

Why do you mend your breast-pleat
    With a rusty needle's thread
And fall with fears and silent tears
    Upon your single bed?

Why do you sit so sadly
    Your face the colour of clay
And with a green gauze handkerchief
    Wipe the sour sweat away?

Has she gone to Blisland
  To seek an easier place,
And is that why your eye won't dry
  And blinds your bleaching face?

'Take me home!' cried Charlotte,
  I lie here in the pit!
A red rock rests upon my breasts
  And my naked neck is split!'

Her skin was soft as sable,
  Her eyes were wide as day,
Her hair was blacker than the bog
  That licked her life away.

Her cheeks were made of honey,
  Her throat was made of flame
Where all around the razor
  Had written its red name.

As Matthew turned at Plymouth
  About the tilting Hoe,
The cold and cunning constable
  Up to him did go:

'I've come to take you, Matthew,
  Unto the magistrate's door.
Come quiet now, you pretty poor boy,
  And you must know what for.'

'She is as pure,' cried Matthew,
  'As is the early dew,
Her only stain it is the pain
  That round her neck I drew!

'She is as guiltless as the day
  She sprang forth from her mother.
The only sin upon her skin
  Is that she loved another.'

They took him off to Bodmin,
    They pulled the prison bell,
They sent him smartly up to heaven
    And dropped him down to hell.

All through the granite kingdom
    And on its travelling airs
Ask which of these two lovers
    The most deserves your prayers.

And your steel heart search, Stranger,
    That you may pause and pray
For lovers who come not to bed
    Upon their wedding day,

But lie upon the moorland
    Where stands the sacred snow
Above the breathing river,
    And the salt sea-winds go.

Cowboy Song

I come from Salem County
    Where the silver melons grow,
Where the wheat is sweet as an angel's feet
    And the zithering zephyrs blow.
I walk the blue bone-orchard
    In the apple-blossom snow,
When the teasy bees take their honeyed ease
    And the marmalade moon hangs low.

My Maw sleeps prone on the prairie
    In a boulder eiderdown,
Where the pickled stars in their little jam-jars
    Hang in a hoop to town.
I haven't seen Paw since a Sunday
    In eighteen seventy-three
When he packed his snap in a bitty mess-trap
    And said he'd be home by tea.

Fled is my fancy sister
  All weeping like the willow,
And dead is the brother I loved like no other
  Who once did share my pillow.
I fly the florid water
  Where run the seven geese round,
O the townsfolk talk to see me walk
  Six inches off the ground.

Across the map of midnight
  I trawl the turning sky,
In my green glass the salt fleets pass
  The moon her fire-float by.
The girls go gay in the valley
  When the boys come down from the farm,
Don't run, my joy, from a poor cowboy,
  I won't do you no harm.

The bread of my twentieth birthday
  I buttered with the sun,
Though I sharpen my eyes with lovers' lies
  I'll never see twenty-one.
Light is my shirt with lilies,
  And lined with lead my hood,
On my face as I pass is a plate of brass,
  And my suit is made of wood.

Death Of A Poet

Suddenly his mouth filled with sand.
His tractor of blood stopped thumping.
He held five icicles in each hand.
His heart packed up jumping.

His face turned the colour of something forgotten in the larder.
His thirty-two teeth were expelled on the kitchen floor.
His muscles, at long last, got considerably harder.
He felt younger than he had for some time before.

Four heroes, steady as wrestlers, each carried him on a shoulder
Into a great grey church laid out like a brain.
 An iron bowl sent out stiff rays of chrysanthemums. It grew colder.
The sun, as expected, failed to break through the pane.

The parson boomed like a dockyard gun at a christening.
Somebody read from the bible. It seemed hours.
I got the feeling you were curled up inside the box, listening.
There was the thud of hymn-books, the stench of flowers.

I remembered hearing your voice on a bloody foment
Of Atlantic waters. The words burned clear as a flare.
Life begins, you said, *as of this moment*.
A bird flew down out of the hurling air.

Over the church a bell broke like a wave upended.
The hearse left for winter with a lingering hiss.
I looked in the wet sky for a sign, but no bird descended.
I went across the road to the pub; wrote this.

Song Of The Dying Gunner A.A. 1

Oh mother my mouth is full of stars
As cartridges in the tray
My blood is a twin-branched scarlet tree
And it runs all runs away.

Oh 'Cooks to the galley' is sounded off
And the lads are down in the mess
But I lie done by the forrard gun
With a bullet in my breast.

Don't send me a parcel at Christmas time
Of socks and nutty and wine
And don't depend on a long weekend
By the Great Western Railway line.

Farewell, Aggie Weston, the Barracks at Guz,
Hang my tiddley suit on the door
I'm sewn up neat in a canvas sheet
And I shan't be home no more.

HMS Glory

Convoy

Draw the blanket of ocean
Over the frozen face.
He lies, his eyes quarried by glittering fish,
Staring through the green freezing sea-glass
At the Northern Lights.

He is now a child in the land of Christmas:
Watching, amazed, the white tumbling bears
And the diving seal.
The iron wind clangs round the ice-caps,
The five-pointed Dog-star
Burns over the silent sea,

And the three ships
Come sailing in.

Death Of An Aircraft
An incident of the Cretan campaign, 1941

To George Psychoundakis

One day on our village in the month of July
An aeroplane sank from the sea of the sky,
    White as a whale it smashed on the shore
    Bleeding oil and petrol all over the floor.

The Germans advanced in the vertical heat
To save the dead plane from the people of Crete,
    And round the glass wreck in a circus of snow
    Set seven mechanical sentries to go.

Seven stalking spiders about the sharp sun
Clicking like clockwork and each with a gun,
    But at 'Come to the cookhouse' they wheeled about
    And sat down to sausages and *sauerkraut*.

Down from the mountain burning so brown
Wriggled three heroes from Kastelo town,
    Deep in the sand they silently sank
    And each struck a match for a petrol tank.

Up went the plane in a feather of fire
As the bubbling boys began to retire
    And, grey in the guardhouse, seven Berliners
    Lost their stripes as well as their dinners.

Down in the village, at murder-stations,
The Germans fell in friends and relations:
    But not a Kastelian snapped an eye
    As he spat in the air and prepared to die.

Not a Kastelian whispered a word
Dressed with the dust to be massacred,
    And squinted up at the sky with a frown
    As three bubbly boys came walking down.

One was sent to the county gaol
Too young for bullets if not for bail,
    But the other two were in prime condition
    To take on a load of ammunition.

In Archontiki they stood in the weather
Naked, hungry, chained together:
    Stark as the stones in the market-place,
    Under the eyes of the populace.

Their irons unlocked as their naked hearts
They faced the squad and their funeral-carts.
    The Captain cried, 'Before you're away
    Is there any last word you'd like to say?'

'I want no words,' said one, 'with my lead,
Only some water to cool my head.'
    'Water,' the other said,' 's all very fine
    But I'll be taking a glass of wine.

'A glass of wine for the afternoon
With permission to sing a signature tune!'
    And he ran the *raki* down his throat
    And he took a deep breath for the leading note.

But before the squad could shoot or say
Like an impala he leapt away
   Over the rifles, under the biers,
   The bullets rattling round his ears.

'Run!' they cried to the boy of stone
Who now stood there in the street alone,
   But, 'Rather than bring revenge on your head
   It is better for me to die,' he said.

The soldiers turned their machine-guns round
And shot him down with a dreadful sound
   Scrubbed his face with perpetual dark
   And rubbed it out like a pencil mark.

But his comrade slept in the olive tree
And sailed by night on the gnawing sea,
   The soldier's silver shilling earned
   And, armed like an archangel, returned.

Ted Hughes

The Thought-Fox

I imagine this midnight moment's forest:
Something else is alive
Besides the clock's loneliness
And this blank page where my fingers move.

Through the window I see no star:
Something more near
Though deeper within darkness
Is entering the loneliness:

Cold, delicately as the dark snow,
A fox's nose touches twig, leaf;
Two eyes serve a movement, that now
And again now, and now, and now

Sets neat prints into the snow
Between trees, and warily a lame
Shadow lags by stump and in hollow
Of a body that is bold to come

Across clearings, an eye,
A widening deepening greenness,
Brilliantly, concentratedly,
Coming about its own business

Till, with a sudden sharp hot stink of fox
It enters the dark hole of the head.
The window is starless still: the clock ticks,
The page is printed.

Wind

This house has been far out at sea all night,
The woods crashing through darkness, the booming hills,
Winds stampeding the fields under the window
Floundering black astride and blinding wet

Till day rose; then under an orange sky
The hills had new places, and wind wielded
Blade-light, luminous and emerald.
Flexing like the lens of a mad eye.

At noon I scaled along the house-side as far as
The coal-house door. I dared once to look up—
Through the brunt wind that dented the balls of my eyes
The tent of the hills drummed and strained its guyrope,

The fields quivering, the skyline a grimace,
At any second to bang and vanish with a flap:
The wind flung a magpie away and a black-
Back gull bent like an iron bar slowly. The house

Rang like some fine green goblet in the note
That any second would shatter it. Now deep
In chairs, in front of the great fire, we grip
Our hearts and cannot entertain book, thought,

Or each other. We watch the fire blazing,
And feel the roots of the house move, but sit on,
Seeing the windows tremble to come in,
Hearing the stones cry out under the horizons.

November

The month of the drowned dog. After long rain the land
Was sodden as the bed of an ancient lake,
Treed with iron and birdless. In the sunk lane
The ditch—a seep silent all summer—

Made brown foam with a big voice: that, and my boots
On the lane's scrubbed stones, in the gulleyed leaves,
Against the hill's hanging silence;
Mist silvering the droplets on the bare thorns

Slower than the change of daylight.
In a let of the ditch a tramp was bundled asleep:
Face tucked down into beard, drawn in
Under its hair like a hedgehog's. I took him for dead,

But his stillness separated from the death
Of the rotting grass and the ground. A wind chilled,
And a fresh comfort tightened through him,
Each hand stuffed deeper into the other sleeve.

His ankles, bound with sacking and hairy band,
Rubbed each other, resettling. The wind hardened;
A puff shook a glittering from the thorns,
And again the rains' dragging grey columns

Smudged the farms. In a moment
The fields were jumping and smoking; the thorns
Quivered, riddled with the glassy verticals.
I stayed on under the welding cold

Watching the tramp's face glisten and the drops on his coat
Flash and darken. I thought what strong trust
Slept in him—as the trickling furrows slept,
And the thorn-roots in their grip on darkness;

And the buried stones, taking the weight of winter;
The hill where the hare crouched with clenched teeth.
Rain plastered the land till it was shining
Like hammered lead, and I ran, and in the rushing wood

Shuttered by a black oak leaned.
The keeper's gibbet had owls and hawks
By the neck, weasels, a gang of cats, crows:
Some, stiff, weightless, twirled like dry bark bits

In the drilling rain. Some still had their shape,
Had their pride with it; hung, chins on chests,
Patient to outwait these worst days that beat
Their crowns bare and dripped from their feet.

Crow Hill

The farms are oozing craters in
Sheer sides under the sodden moors:
When it is not wind it is rain,
Neither of which will stop at doors:
One will damp beds and the other shake
Dreams beneath sleep it cannot break.

Beneath the weather and the rock
Farmers make a little heat;
Cows that sway a bony back,
Pigs upon delicate feet
Hold off the sky, trample the strength
That shall level these hills at length.

Buttoned from the blowing mist
Walk the ridges of ruined stone.
What humbles these hills has raised
The arrogance of blood and bone,
And thrown the hawk upon the wind,
And lit the fox in the dripping ground.

Hawk Roosting

I sit in the top of the wood, my eyes closed.
Inaction, no falsfying dream
Between my hooked head and hooked feet:
Or in a sleep rehearse perfect kills and eat.

The convenience of the high trees!
The air's buoyancy and the sun's ray
Are of advantage to me;
And the earth's face upward for my inspection.

My feet are locked upon the rough bark.
It took the whole of Creation
To produce my foot, my each feather:
Now I hold Creation in my foot

Or fly up, and revolve it all slowly—
I kill where I please because it is all mine.
There is no sophistry in my body:
My manners are tearing off heads—

The allotment of death.
For the one path of my flight is direct
Through the bones of the living.
No arguments assert my right:

The sun is behind me.
Nothing has changed since I began.
My eye has permitted no change.
I am going to keep things like this.

Thrushes

Terrifying are the attent sleek thrushes on the lawn,
More coiled steel than living—a poised
Dark deadly eye, those delicate legs
Triggered to stirrings beyond sense—with a start, a bounce, a stab
Overtake the instant and drag out some writhing thing.
No indolent procrastinations and no yawning stares,
No sighs or head-scratchings. Nothing but bounce and stab
And a ravening second.

Is it their single-mind-sized skulls, or a trained
Body, or genius, or a nestful of brats
Gives their days this bullet and automatic
Purpose? Mozart's brain had it, and the shark's mouth
That hungers down the blood-smell even to a leak of its own
Side and devouring of itself: efficiency which
Strikes too streamlined for any doubt to pluck at it
Or obstruction deflect.

With a man it is otherwise. Heroisms on horseback,
Outstripping his desk-diary at a broad desk,
Carving at a tiny ivory ornament
For years: his act worships itself—while for him,
Though he bends to be blent in the prayer, how loud and above
what
Furious spaces of fire do the distracting devils
Orgy and hosannah, under what wilderness
Of black silent waters weep.

Esther's Tomcat

Daylong this tomcat lies stretched flat
As an old rough mat, no mouth and no eyes.
Continual wars and wives are what
Have tattered his ears and battered his head.

Like a bundle of old rope and iron
Sleeps till blue dusk. Then reappear
His eyes, green as ringstones: he yawns wide red,
Fangs fine as a lady's needle and bright.

A tomcat sprang at a mounted knight,
Locked round his neck like a trap of hooks
While the knight rode fighting its clawing and bite.
After hundreds of years the stain's there

On the stone where he fell, dead of the tom:
That was at Barnborough. The tomcat still
Grallochs odd dogs on the quiet,
Will take the head clean off your simple pullet,

Is unkillable. From the dog's fury,
From gunshot fired point-blank he brings
His skin whole, and whole
From owlish moons of bekittenings

Among ashcans. He leaps and lightly
Walks upon sleep, his mind on the moon.
Nightly over the round world of men,
Over the roofs go his eyes and outcry.

Pike

Pike, three inches long, perfect
Pike in all parts, green tigering the gold.
Killers from the egg: the malevolent aged grin.
They dance on the surface among the flies.

Or move, stunned by their own grandeur,
Over a bed of emerald, silhouette
Of submarine delicacy and horror.
A hundred feet long in their world.

In ponds, under the heat-struck lily pads—
Gloom of their stillness:
Logged on last year's black leaves, watching upwards.
Or hung in an amber cavern of weeds

The jaws' hooked clamp and fangs
Not to be changed at this date;
A life subdued to its instrument;
The gills kneading quietly, and the pectorals.

Three we kept behind glass,
Jungled in weed: three inches, four,
And four and a half: fed fry to them—
Suddenly there were two. Finally one

With a sag belly and the grin it was born with.
And indeed they spare nobody.
Two, six pounds each, over two feet long,
High and dry and dead in the willow-herb—

One jammed past its gills down the other's gullet:
The outside eye stared: as a vice locks—
The same iron in this eye
Though its film shrank in death.

A pond I fished, fifty yards across,
Whose lilies and muscular tench
Had outlasted every visible stone
Of the monastery that planted them—

Stilled legendary depth:
It was as deep as England. It held
Pike too immense to stir, so immense and old
That past nightfall I dared not cast

But silently cast and fished
With the hair frozen on my head
For what might move, for what eye might move.
The still splashes on the dark pond,

Owls hushing the floating woods
Frail on my ear against the dream
Darkness beneath night's darkness had freed,
That rose slowly towards me, watching.

Snowdrop

Now is the globe shrunk tight
Round the mouse's dulled wintering heart.
Weasel and crow, as if moulded in brass,
Move through an outer darkness
Not in their right minds,
With the other deaths. She, too, pursues her ends,
Brutal as the stars of this month,
Her pale head heavy as metal.

Her Husband

Comes home dull with coal-dust deliberately
To grime the sink and foul towels and let her
Learn with scrubbing brush and scrubbing board
The stubborn character of money.

And let her learn through what kind of dust
He has earned his thirst and the right to quench it
And what sweat he has exchanged for his money
And the blood-weight of money. He'll humble her

With new light on her obligations.
The fried, woody chips, kept warm two hours in the oven,
Are only part of her answer.
Hearing the rest, he slams them to the fire back

And is away round the house-end singing
'Come back to Sorrento' in a voice
Of resounding corrugated iron.
Her back has bunched into a hump as an insult.

For they will have their rights.
Their jurors are to be assembled.
From the little crumbs of soot. Their brief
Goes straight up to heaven and nothing more is heard of it.

Thistles

Against the rubber tongues of cows and the hoeing hands of men
Thistles spike the summer air
Or crackle open under a blue-black pressure.

Every one a revengeful burst
Of resurrection, a grasped fistful
Of splintered weapons and Icelandic frost thrust up

From the underground stain of a decayed Viking.
They are like pale hair and the gutturals of dialects.
Every one manages a plume of blood.

Then they grow grey, like men.
Mown down, it is a feud. Their sons appear,
Stiff with weapons, fighting back over the same ground.

Bayonet Charge

Suddenly he awoke and was running—raw
In raw-seamed hot khaki, his sweat heavy,
Stumbling across a field of clods towards a green hedge
That dazzled with rifle fire, hearing
Bullets smacking the belly out of the air—
He lugged a rifle numb as a smashed arm;
The patriotic tear that had brimmed in his eye
Sweating like molten iron from the center of his chest,—

In bewilderment then he almost stopped—
In what cold clockwork of the stars and the nations
Was he the hand pointing that second? He was running
Like a man who has jumped up in the dark and runs
Listening between his footfalls for the reason
Of his still running, and his foot hung like
Statuary in mid-stride. Then the shot-slashed furrows

Threw up a yellow hare that rolled like a flame
And crawled in a threshing circle, its mouth wide
Open silent, its eyes standing out.
He plunged past with his bayonet toward the green hedge.
King, honour, human dignity, etcetera
Dropped like luxuries in a yelling alarm
To get out of that blue crackling air
His terror's touchy dynamite.

Six Young Men

The celluloid of a photograph holds them well,—
Six young men, familiar to their friends.
Four decades that have faded and ochre-tinged
This photograph have not wrinkled the faces or the hands.
Though their cocked hats are not now fashionable,
Their shoes shine. One imparts an intimate smile,
One chews a grass, one lowers his eyes, bashful,
One is ridiculous with cocky pride—
Six months after this picture they were all dead.

All are trimmed for a Sunday jaunt. I know
That bilberried bank, that thick tree, that black wall,
Which are there yet and not changed. From where these sit
You hear the water of seven streams fall
To the roarer in the bottom, and through all
The leafy valley a rumouring of air go.
Pictured here, their expressions listen yet,
And still that valley has not changed its sound
Though their faces are four decades under the ground.

This one was shot in an attack and lay
Calling in the wire, then this one, his best friend,
Went out to bring him in and was shot too;
And this one, the very moment he was warned
From potting at tin-cans in no-man's-land,
Fell back dead with his rifle-sights shot away.
The rest, nobody knows what they came to,
But come to the worst they must have done, and held it
Closer than their hope; all were killed.

Here see a man's photograph,
The locket of a smile, turned overnight
Into the hospital of his mangled last
Agony and hours; see bundled in it
His mightier-than-a-man dead bulk and weight:
And on this one place which keeps him alive
(In his Sunday best) see fall war's worst
Thinkable flash and rending, onto his smile
Forty years rotting into soil.

That man's not more alive whom you confront
And shake by the hand, see hale, hear speak loud,
Than any of these six celluloid smiles are,
Nor prehistoric or fabulous beast more dead;
No thought so vivid as their smoking blood:
To regard this photograph might well dement,
Such contradictory permanent horrors here
Smile from the single exposure and shoulder out
One's own body from its instant and heat.

Dick Straightup

Past eighty, but never in eighty years—
Eighty winters on the windy ridge
Of England—has he buttoned his shirt or his jacket.
He sits in the bar-room seat he has been
Polishing with his backside sixty-odd years
Where nobody else sits. White is his head,
But his cheek high, hale as when he emptied
Every Saturday the twelve-pint tankard at a tilt,
Swallowed the whole serving of thirty eggs,
And banged the big brass drum for Heptonstall—
With a hundred other great works, still talked of.
Age has stiffened him, but not dazed or bent,˙
The blue eye has come clear of time:
At a single pint, now, his memory sips slowly,
His belly strong as a tree bole.

He survives among hills, nourished by stone and height.
The dust of Achilles and Cuchulain
Itches in the palms of scholars; thin clerks exercise
In their bed-sitters at midnight, and the meat salesman can
Loft fully four hundred pounds. But this one,
With no more application than sitting,
And drinking, and singing, fell in the sleet, late,
Damned the pouring gutter; and slept there; and, throughout
A night searched by shouts and lamps, froze,
Grew to the road with welts of ice. He was chipped out at dawn
Warm as a pie and snoring.

The gossip of men younger by forty years—
Loud in his company since he no longer says much—
Empties, refills and empties their glasses.
Or their strenuous silence places the dominoes
(That are old as the house) into patterns
Gone with the game; the darts that glint to the dartboard
Pin no remarkable instant. The young men sitting
Taste their beer as by imitation,
Borrow their words as by impertinence
Because he sits there so full of legend and life
Quiet as a man alone.

He lives with sixty and seventy years ago,
And of everything he knows three quarters is in the grave,
Or tumbled down, or vanished. To be understood
His words must tug up the bottom-most stones of this village,
This clutter of blackstone gulleys, peeping curtains,
And a graveyard bigger and deeper than the village
That sways in the tide of wind and rain some fifty
Miles off the Irish sea.
                            The lamp above the pub-door
Wept yellow when he went out and the street
Of spinning darkness roared like a machine
As the wind applied itself. His upright walk,
His strong back, I commemorate now,
And his white blown head going out between a sky and an earth
That were bundled into placeless blackness, the one
Company of his mind.

Obit.

Now, you are strong as the earth you have entered.

This is a birthplace picture. Green into blue
The hills run deep and limpid. The weasel's
Berry-eyed red lock-head, gripping the dream
That holds good, goes lost in the heaved calm

Of the earth you have entered.

The Bull Moses

A hoist up and I could lean over
The upper edge of the high half-door,
My left foot ledged on the hinge, and look in at the byre's
Blaze of darkness: a sudden shut-eyed look
Backward into the head.
                            Blackness is depth
Beyond star. But the warm weight of his breathing,
The ammoniac reek of his litter, the hotly-tongued
Mash of his cud, steamed against me.
Then, slowly, as onto the mind's eye—
The brow like masonry, the deep-keeled neck:

Something come up there onto the brink of the gulf,
Hadn't heard of the world, too deep in itself to be called to,
Stood in sleep. He would swing his muzzle at a fly
But the square of sky where I hung, shouting, waving,
Was nothing to him; nothing of our light
Found any reflection in him.
                   Each dusk the farmer led him
Down to the pond to drink and smell the air,
And he took no pace but the farmer
Led him to take it, as if he knew nothing
Of the ages and continents of his fathers,
Shut, while he wombed, to a dark shed
And steps between his door and the duckpond;
The weight of the sun and the moon and the world hammered
To a ring of brass through his nostrils.
                 He would raise
His streaming muzzle and look out over the meadows,
But the grasses whispered nothing awake, the fetch
Of the distance drew nothing to momentum
In the locked black of his powers. He came strolling gently back,
Paused neither toward the pig-pens on his right,
Nor toward the cow-byres on his left: something
Deliberate in his leisure, some beheld future
Founding in his quiet.
            I kept the door wide,
Closed it after him and pushed the bolt.

The Horses

I climbed through woods in the hour-before-dawn dark.
Evil air, a frost-making stillness,

Not a leaf, not a bird,—
A world cast in frost. I came out above the wood

Where my breath left tortuous statues in the iron light.
But the valleys were draining the darkness

Till the moorline—blackening dregs of the brightening grey—
Halved the sky ahead. And I saw the horses:

Huge in the dense grey—ten together—
Megalith-still. They breathed, making no move,

With draped manes and tilted hind-hooves,
Making no sound.

I passed: not one snorted or jerked its head.
Grey silent fragments

Of a grey silent world.

I listened in emptiness on the moor-ridge.
The curlew's tear turned its edge on the silence.

Slowly detail leafed from the darkness. Then the sun
Orange, red, red, erupted

Silently, and splitting to its core tore and flung cloud,
Shook the gulf open, showed blue,

And the big planets hanging—.
I turned

Stumbling in the fever of a dream, down towards
The dark woods, from the kindling tops,

And came to the horses.
                              There, still they stood,
But now steaming and glistening under the flow of light,

Their draped stone manes, their tilted hind-hooves
Stirring under a thaw while all around them

The frost showed its fires. But still they made no sound.
Not one snorted or stamped,

Their hung heads patient as the horizons,
High over valleys, in the red levelling rays—

In din of the crowded streets, going among the years, the faces,
May I still meet my memory in so lonely a place

Between the streams and the red clouds, hearing curlews,
Hearing the horizons endure.

Some Starting Points For Discussion

Thomas Hardy (1840–1928)

Thomas Hardy, born near Dorchester, the son of a stone-mason, began a career as architect, but by nature and choice was a poet, believing that 'in verse was contained the essence of all imaginative and emotional literature'. For a quarter of a century he wrote novels as a 'temporary' but economically 'compulsory' interruption of his poetic career, and his first volume of poems, a selection of the previous thirty years' writing, was published when he was 58, followed by seven more volumes between 1902 and 1928. His Collected Poems (published 1930) contained 920 poems composed over more than sixty years. An extensive selection (ed. Creighton) was published by Macmillan in 1974.

1   **The Darkling Thrush**
    (a) Why 'darkling'? Look carefully at the details of this poem's setting—the landscape, the weather, the time of year—and discuss the implications of the scene they form. What do they suggest of the poet's feelings?
    (b) What is Hardy's attitude towards the singing bird? (Compare Keats' *Ode To A Nightingale* and Shelley's *To A Skylark*—you can find both in the *Oxford Book Of English Verse*: do you think Hardy had these poems in mind when writing *The Darkling Thrush*?).
    (c) Listen to the sounds of the words when spoken aloud and the poem's rhymes and rhythm: is the poet's 'song' 'fervourless', or, like the 'aged thrush', 'ecstatic'?
    (d) What is contributed to the total effect of the poem by the imagery:
      'spectre-gray', 'Winter's dregs', 'scored . . . Like strings of broken lyres', 'The Century's corpse *outleant*. . . .'
    Why use an archaic word here? Can you find further examples in other poems included in this selection?
    (e) Compare R. S. Thomas, *The Lonely Farmer*.

2   **Afterwards/An August Midnight/At Middle-field Gate In February**
    (a) Compare the picture of Hardy that emerges in *Afterwards* with the image you formed of him when reading *The Darkling Thrush*.
    (b) 'A man who used to notice such things': look carefully at the details of nature Hardy 'notices' and the words he has chosen to imagine them. Read the first two stanzas of *At Middle-field Gate in February* aloud: how do the sounds of the words and the rhythm of the lines help us to imagine the scene they describe?
    (c) Compare Robert Graves, *Lost Love*.

163

3   **The Self Unseeing/A Night In November/A Thunderstorm In Town/Beyond The Last Lamp**
(a) In what ways are these poems similar and how do they differ?
(b) Why does Hardy find an apparently humdrum encounter to be of deep significance in *Beyond The Last Lamp*?
How do other poems in this selection echo the mood of this poem?
(c)   'Stanza forms endlessly varied and inventive are always part of the meaning they convey, not superimposed on it, and declare why they are so and not otherwise. The number of lines in a stanza modifies its expressiveness. Relations between lines of similar or different lengths always say something.' (T. M. R. Creighton)
How do the stanza forms affect what is 'said' by these poems?

4   **The Voice/After A Journey/At Castle Boterel**
(a) These poems were written after a visit Hardy made alone to the coast of North Cornwall (the setting of many of Charles Causley's poems and John Betjeman's *Winter Seascape*) during the year following his wife's death, 1912–13. Read them as a sequence and discuss what they add to the impressions of Hardy you have formed previously.
(b) Read the following comments Hardy made about poetry and discuss their relevance to these poems:
  'The ultimate aim of the poet should be to touch our hearts by showing his own';
  'The business of the poet and novelist is to show the sorriness underlying the grandest things, and the grandeur underlying the sorriest things';
  'Poetry is emotion put into measure. The emotion must come by nature, but the measure can be acquired by art'.
Do you think that the other poets included in this anthology would agree with the opinions expressed here?
(c) Pay particular attention to the rhythms of these poems: how do they help to convey Hardy's 'emotion'?

5   **Silences/Old Furniture**
(a)   '. . . For my part, if there is any way of getting a melancholy satisfaction out of life, it lies in dying, so to speak, before one is out of the flesh; by which I mean putting on the manners of ghosts, wandering in their haunts, and taking their views of surrounding things. To think of life as passing away is a sadness; to think of it as past is at least tolerable. Hence even when I enter into a room to pay a simple morning call I have unconsciously the habit of regarding the scene as if I were a spectre not solid enough to influence my environment; only fit to behold and say, as another spectre said: "Peace be unto you!"'.'
Compare the 'ghosts' of these poems with those that appear in *The Voice*, etc (4 above). Have you had similar experiences to those described here?
(b) Discuss the effect of the short lines in *Old Furniture*, comparing Hardy's use of long and short lines and varying stanza forms in other poems in this selection—how does the 'shape' of a poem help to convey its meaning?
(c) Compare *Old Furniture* with *The Pier Glass*, by Robert Graves.

6   **During Wind And Rain**
(a) Compare this poem with *The Darkling Thrush*.
(b) Discuss your reactions to the images in the last line of each stanza, and

the repetition of 'Ah no the years o'. How is Hardy's concern with the
passing of time expressed in the other poems in this selection? How do his
references to the seasons help to convey this concern?

7 **In Time Of 'The Breaking Of Nations'**
(a) Hardy lived through the First World War (in which Wilfred Owen was
killed). What do the three images presented here tell us of Hardy's attitude
towards historic events?
(b) Compare this poem with *Musée Des Beaux Arts*, by W. H. Auden.
(c) What do you think Hardy felt to be important in life? (Include the other
poems of this selection in your discussion as well.)

8 **He Never Expected Much**
   'As, in looking at a carpet, by following one colour a certain pattern is
suggested, by following another colour, another; so in life the seer should
watch that pattern among general things which his idiosyncrasy moves him to
observe, and describe that alone. This is, quite accurately, a going to Nature;
yet the result is no mere photograph, but purely the product of the writer's
own mind.'
   Use this poem as the starting-point for a discussion of the impressions you
have formed of Hardy as a person through reading his poetry and the
'pattern' it describes.

Wilfred Owen (1893–1918)

Owen enlisted in 1915. During the winter of 1916–17, one of the hardest winters
of this century, he was with the Lancashire Fusiliers in the front line on the
Somme. The following extracts are from letters he wrote to his mother:
   'We are now a long way back, in a ruined village, all huddled together in a
farm. We all sleep in the same room where we eat and try to live. My bed is a
hammock of rabbit-wire stuck up beside a great shell-hole in the wall. Snow is
deep about, and melts through the gaping roof, on to my blanket. We are
wretched beyond my previous imagination—but safe. Last night indeed I had
to "go up" with a party. We got lost in the snow. I went on ahead to
scout—foolishly alone—and, when half a mile away from the party, got
overtaken by

GAS.

It was only tear-gas from a shell, and I got safely back (to the party) in my
helmet, with nothing worse than a severe fright! And a few tears, some natural,
some unnatural. . . . Coal, water, candles, accommodation, everything is
scarce. We have not always air! When I took my helmet off last night—O Air, it
was a heavenly thing! . . . They want to call No Man's Land "England" because
we keep supremacy there. . . . It is pock-marked like a body of foulest disease,
and its odour is the breath of cancer. I have not seen any dead. I have done
worse. In the dank air I have *perceived* it, and in the darkness, *felt*. . . . No Man's
Land under snow is like the face of the moon, chaotic, crater-ridden,
uninhabitable, awful, the abode of madness. To call it "England"! . . .'

   'In this place my platoon had no dug-outs, but had to lie in the snow under
the deadly wind. By day it was impossible to stand up, or even crawl about,

because we were behind only a little ridge screening us from the Boche's periscope. We had 5 Tommy's Cookers between the platoon, but they did not suffice to melt the ice in the water-cans. Se we suffered cruelly from thirst. The marvel is that we did not all die of cold. As a matter of fact, only one of my party actually froze to death before he could be got back, but I am not able to tell how many have ended in hospital. . . . I cannot say I felt any fear. We were all half-crazed by the buffeting of the high explosives. I think the most unpleasant reflection that weighed on me was the impossibility of getting back any wounded. . . . We were marooned in a frozen desert. . . .'

The first poem in this selection is dated February 1917.

1 **Exposure**
(a) Discuss the picture of war that is presented here, and the poet's attitude towards it.
(b) What do you understand by:
'Low, drooping flares confuse our memories of the salient';
'Worried by silence . . .';
'. . . like a dull rumour of some other war';
'Slowly our ghosts drag home';
'For hours the innocent mice rejoice'?
(c) Pay close attention to the last two stanzas: what contrasts do they present?
(d) How is the meaning you have discussed reinforced by the poem's form? Discuss Owen's use of very long lines, and the effect of the short ones that end each stanza; notice also the para-rhymes (e.g. 'burn' 'born')—why not complete rhymes as in other poems?
(e) What is 'poetic' in his description of bullets and snow?—
'Sudden successive flights of bullets streak the silence
Less deadly than the air that shudders black with snow,
With sidelong flowing flakes that flock, pause, and renew. . . .
Pale flakes with fingering stealth come feeling for our faces'.
(f) What is similar in the metaphors he uses to describe the wind (in the second stanza) and the dawn (in the third)?
(g) Compare *The Darkling Thrush*: has Own used *his* landscape in a way similar to Hardy?

2 **Dulce Et Decorum Est** (a reference to the Roman poet Horace—'It is sweet and proper to die for the fatherland')/**Futility/Anthem For Doomed Youth/The Sentry/Apologia Pro Poemate Meo**
(a) 'My subject is war, and the pity of war. The poetry is in the pity'. Discuss how these poems convey Owen's compassion for others who suffered his experience of war. Do the poems express other feelings also?
(b) Each poem presents at least one contrast. Identify the contrasts that you have noticed: do the poems contrast with one another also?
(c) What do you understand the last stanza of *Apologia* to mean?
(d) 'O what made fatuous sunbeams toil
To break earth's sleep at all?' (*Futility*)
Why does the poet call sunbeams 'fatuous'? How are these lines echoed in other poems in this selection?
(e) Other writers (for instance, Robert Graves in *Goodbye To All That* and Ernest Hemingway in *A Farewell To Arms*) have expressed their reactions to the First World War in prose. Could the experiences that formed the basis of these

poems have been as powerfully evoked in short stories? Discuss the particular effects of Owen's choosing verse as his medium of expression—how are the experiences made vivid by his poetry?

3 **Insensibility**
(a) What does Owen admire in the soldiers he refers to in this poem? Are there instances of these qualities in the other poems in this selection, or do they present a differing view?
(b) Does the contrast expressed in this poem resemble that of any of the poems you have discussed previously?
(c) In a letter Owen wrote 'My senses are charred'. Discuss the relevance of this statement to this poem (and others, e.g. *Exposure*). Were his senses numbed by the war? Consider lines like the following:
    'Dim through the misty panes and thick green light,
    As under a green sea, I saw him drowning'   (*Dulce Et Decorum Est*)
    'Only the stuttering rifles' rapid rattle
    Can patter out their hasty orisons'   (*Anthem For Doomed Youth*)
    'Rain, guttering down in waterfalls of slime
    Kept slush waist-high that, rising hour by hour,
    Choked up the steps too thick with clay to climb'   (*The Sentry*)
(d) Compare this poem with *Recalling War*, by Robert Graves and *Six Young Men* by Ted Hughes.

4 **The Send-Off**
(a) How would you describe the atmosphere of this poem? Look carefully at individual words and phrases and discuss the effects they have on the poem and your response to it. Is their meaning clear-cut?
(b) Discuss the various meanings of the following phrases in the context of this poem:
    'grimly gay'; 'As men's are, dead'; 'unmoved'; 'winked'; 'like wrongs hushed up'; 'They were not ours'.

5 **Strange Meeting**
(a) Is this poem about 'the pity of war'?
(b) Discuss the implications of 'I am the enemy you killed, my friend' and 'Let us sleep now'.
(c) The poet, George Macbeth, has written of Owen:
    'In his best poems . . . he writes not only about war but about war as a metaphor for the human condition. This gives his best work a far-reaching gravity and moral force which makes his poems applicable to any situation in which people must suffer and die.'
What is Owen saying in this poem about the 'human condition'?
(d) Where is the 'Hell' of this poem?
(e) Are Owen's poems generally merely descriptions of other 'strange meetings', memorable events that he has kept alive for us through the power of his writing, or do the experiences refer to more than themselves?
(f) How would you describe Owen's attitude to war as shown in these poems? What does this attitude tell us of the poet's attitude to life?
Owen was invalided home in the summer of 1917, and met Siegfried Sassoon (who had published many poems, and whose encouragement was greatly valued by Owen) and Robert Graves. Before going to hospital, Owen had written in a letter home:

'Already I have comprehended as light which will never filter into the dogma of any national church: namely that one of Christ's essential commands was, Passivity at any price! Suffer dishonour and disgrace, but never resort to arms. Be bullied, be outraged, be killed; but do not kill . . . Christ is literally in no man's land. There men often hear his voice. Greater love hath no man than this, that a man lay down his life—for a friend. Is it spoken in English only and French? I do not believe so. Thus you see how pure Christianity will not fit in with pure patriotism.'

Sassoon wrote, in 'A Working Party':

Three hours ago he stumbled up the trench:
Now he will never walk that road again:
He must be carried back, a jolting lump,
Beyond all need of tenderness and care.

and in 'The Death-Bed'

He's young; he hated War; how should he die
When cruel old campaigners win safe through?

His poetry expresses his indignation against warmongers, protesting at the tragedies that occurred daily, unregarded by many at home. The poet C. Day Lewis wrote in the introduction to the *Collected Poems of Wilfred Owen* that

'We shall not fully understand the poetry of protest written by Owen, Sassoon and others, unless we realize how great was the gulf between the fighting man and the civilian at home, and between the front-line soldier and the brass-hat. To the soldier, those on the other side of the barbed wire were fellow-sufferers; he felt less hostility towards them than towards the men and women who were profiting by the war, sheltered from it, or wilfully ignorant of its realities. . . . Wilfred Owen went back to the front line because he would be in a stronger position to voice his protest against the war, and speak for his comrades.'

On 4 October 1918, after most of his company had been killed, he and a lance-corporal captured a German machine gun and scores of prisoners, and was subsequently awarded the M.C. On 4 November (a week before the Armistice) he was killed when trying to construct a make-shift bridge (over which his company could cross the Sambre Canal) in the face of heavy machine-gun fire.

The *Collected Poems* are published by Chatto and Windus. Poems written by other soldiers, including Sassoon and Owen, appear in *1914–18 in Poetry* (ed. Black) published by the University of London Press.

Robert Graves (1895–   )

Graves fought on the Western Front with the Royal Welch Fusiliers for long periods in 1915–17, and was seriously wounded at the Somme. He was a close friend of Sassoon (who was in the same regiment) and later of Owen. On his twenty-first birthday he was reported 'Died of wounds', but he lived to write of his experiences of the war and his reasons for leaving England to live in Majorca (in *Goodbye To All That*, available in a Penguin edition). He is also the author of *I Claudius* and *Claudius, The God* (books about life at court in ancient Rome). His *Collected Poems* and other volumes of poetry are published by Cassell; there is also a Penguin selection (chosen by himself). He was elected Professor of Poetry at Oxford University in 1961.

1 **Rising Early**
   (a) 'Thanks indeed for that': what is Graves grateful for?
   (b) What does Graves ask for at the end of the poem?
   (c) Compare the experience of an early morning described by Ted Hughes in *The Horses*: is it valued for a similar reason?

2 **The Cool Web**
   (a) Discuss the poet's attitude to language presented in this poem: what is the effect of its 'watery clasp' on our reactions to experiences like those mentioned at the beginning of this poem? Can you think of instances when people have used language in this way? Is it important that our tongues keep their 'self-possession'?
   (b) What is meant by 'the wide glare of the children's day' and the last two lines of the third stanza?
   (c) Do the poets in this volume use language to 'spell away' or do they 'face the wide glare'? (For instance, Graves in *Surgical Ward: Men* and *Recalling War*.)

3 **Lost Love**
   (a) Compare this poem with Hardy's poems, especially *Afterwards*.
   (b) Discuss the poet's choice of words to describe the sounds the man can hear, for instance:
      'drinking sound of grass'; 'Whir of spiders'; 'clashing jaws of moth chumbling holes'.
   (c) Why is the man described as 'god-like' or 'like a thief'?

4 **Not At Home**
   (a) Is either of the comparisons referred to in (3c) above appropriate to the narrator of this poem?
   (b) Describe how you think his feelings change as he approaches the house, talks to the gardener, and leaves. How do the details of the house, the weather, and similar features of the poem's setting echo those feelings?
   (c) What impressions of the lady (and of the narrator's feelings towards her) do you form from the description of the house and from the remarks of the gardener?

5 **Welsh Incident/The 'Alice Jean'**
   (a) How would you describe the atmospheres of these poems—sinister?
   (b) Compare the poems' presentations of their 'stories' (cf. also *O What Is That Sound* by W. H. Auden).
   (c) Several of Graves' lighter poems show his interest in monsters; in *Welsh Incident* they are not described—what is the effect of this?

6 **The Haunted House**
   (a) Discuss what you think the image of the haunted house symbolizes: are there any clues in other poems included in this selection, and in the 'clouded tales of wrong and terror' of other poets?
   (b) Who, do you think, is the 'surly fellow'?
   (c) Why has Graves chosen a ballad form instead of an arrangement similar to that of the previous poem? (Compare *As I Walked Out One Evening*, by W. H. Auden and *Innocent's Song* and *Song Of The Dying Gunner*, by Charles Causley.)
   (d) Compare *Order To View* and *Débâcle*, by Louis Macneice.

7   **Surgical Ward: Men**
    (a) Discuss the last two lines of this poem: how is pain 'unpurposed, matchless'? Do your experiences cause you to agree with the comparison of the last line?
    (b) Compare this poem with *Surgical Ward*, by W. H. Auden, and *The Building*, by Philip Larkin.

8   **The Leveller/Recalling War**
    (a) The title of the first poem refers to a poem by James Shirley (1596–1666) called *Death, the Leveller*:

> The glories of our blood and state
>   Are shadows, not substantial things;
> There is no armour against Fate;
>   Death lays his icy hand on kings:
>   Sceptre and Crown
>   Must tumble down,
> And in the dust be equal made
> With the poor crooked scythe and spade.
>
> Some men with swords may reap the field,
>   And plant fresh laurels where they kill:
> But their strong nerves at last must yield;
>   They tame but one another still:
>   Early or late
>   They stoop to fate,
> And must give up their murmuring breath
> When they, pale captives, creep to death.
>
> The garlands wither on your brow;
>   Then boast no more your mighty deeds!
> Upon Death's purple altar now
>   See where the victor-victim bleeds.
>   Your heads must come
>   To the cold tomb:
> Only the actions of the just
> Smell sweet and blossom in their dust.

Discuss the relevance of this poem to your reading of Graves.
    (b) 'What, then, was war?' What is the poet's answer to this question? What is the point made in the last two lines of *Recalling War*?
    (c) Explain the comparisons made with the 'morning traveller' at the end of the first stanza and the child in the last.
    (d) The war recalled by these poems was the same as that described in Wilfred Owen's poetry: compare the two poets' observations of the effects of the war on those men fighting it.
    (e) Compare *Six Young Men*, by Ted Hughes.

9   **The Pier Glass/The Face In The Mirror**
    (a) Compare the reflections imaged in these two poems.
    (b) The second poem is a self-portrait: what further impressions of the poet do you form from reading the poems included in this selection?
    (c) Compare *The Pier Glass* with *Old Furniture* and *The Darkling Thrush* by Thomas Hardy.

(a) Discuss your answers to the questions posed in the last stanza of the first poem.
(b) Why has Graves given his poems these titles?
(c) How does his arrangement of lines and use of rhyme and repetition help to convey the poems' meanings?
(d) Compare *Counting The Beats* with *During Wind And Rain* by Thomas Hardy.

D. H. Lawrence (1885–1930)

Lawrence was the fourth child of a miner. At 13 he won a scholarship to Nottingham High School, which he left for a job with a firm of surgical goods manufacturers at a wage of thirteen shillings a week. He soon abandoned this to become a pupil-teacher; while attending Nottingham University for his teacher's certificate, he began his first novel, *The White Peacock*, which was published by Heinemann (as were all his poems, novels and short stories) in 1911. Subsequently he lived entirely by his writing (apart from a short period as a schoolmaster), travelling extensively in Europe, Australia and America (where he lived for some time in New Mexico, but returned to Europe in 1929, when he became seriously ill and subsequently died of tuberculosis). A fuller selection of his poems, and his short stories and novels are available in Penguin editions.

1 **Piano/The Collier's Wife/At The Window/Brooding Grief**
(a) These poems were written at about the same time as Lawrence's semi-autobiographical novel *Sons and Lovers*. If you have read the novel, discuss the similarities between the incidents in these poems and events in the story.
(b) What impressions do you form of the husband and wife in *The Collier's Wife*? (Compare *Her Husband*, by Ted Hughes.)
(c) Compare Lawrence's use of the ballad form with W. H. Auden's in *O What Is That Sound* and Charles Causley's in *Nursery Rhyme Of Innocence And Experience* and *The Ballad of Charlotte Dymond*.
(d) Compare Lawrence's imaging of leaves in *At The Window* and *Brooding Grief* with *A Night In November* and other poems by Thomas Hardy.

2 **Giorno Dei Morti**
(a) Compare this poem with *Brooding Grief* and *At The Window*. Is it an emotive poem?
(b) Discuss the effects of Lawrence's rhymes and rhythm, the repetition of certain phrases, and his appeal to our senses in depicting this scene. Besides being a novelist and poet, Lawrence was also a painter: do you think this had any significant effect on his writing?

3 **Bat**
(a) Notice Lawrence's mixture of long and short lines, and the repetition and rhythms of this poem: why is his versification here ('free verse') so different from that of the previous poem?
(b) Look closely at the imagery he uses to describe the bat: what does it tell us about his attitude towards the creature?
(c) How does he help us to imagine its flight in lines like
    'Swallows with spools of dark thread sewing the shadows together'
and

'Dark air-life looping
Yet missing the pure loop . . .
A twitch, a twitter, an elastic shudder in flight'?

4 **Snake/Kangaroo/Humming Bird**
(a) Compare Lawrence's use of repetition and long lines here to describe the movement of the snake with the technique you have noticed in *Bat*.
(b) What do these poems tell us about Lawrence's feelings towards Sicily and Australia, and what do they reveal of Lawrence himself?
(c) Is Lawrence's attitude towards the natural world similar to Hardy's?
(d) How do his poems about animals differ from those of Ted Hughes?
(e) Compare *Humming Bird* with Hardy's and Hughes' poems about thrushes. What is the point of 'Luckily for us'?

5 **Bavarian Gentians**
(a) What is the significance of the reference to Persephone?
(b) What is the darkness that this poem emphasizes? Is it the same as that referred to by Ted Hughes in *Pike* and *The Bull Moses*?

6 **Work/Money Madness**
(a) Do you agree with Lawrence's attitude towards work and money, or do you think it sentimental?
(b) Should cities be 'bowers grown out from the busy bodies of people'? Could this happen without 'smashing the machines'—or must they be 'cancelled'?
(c) Do we 'grovel' before money?
(d) 'It's one thing or the other': do you agree with the alternatives posed by the last poem?

W. H. Auden (1907–73)

Auden drove an ambulance and served as stretcher-bearer on the Republican side during the Spanish Civil War, having previously worked as a schoolmaster and in documentary films. He travelled widely in Europe, and visited Iceland and China, which led to collaborating with friends on two books—*Letters from Iceland* (1937) with Louis Macneice, and *Journey to a War* with Christopher Isherwood (whose autobiographical *Lions and Shadows* gives an amusing and affectionate picture of Auden in the thirties). In 1937 he was awarded the King's Medal for Poetry, and in 1938 he emigrated to the USA, subsequently becoming an American citizen. Later in his life he spent long periods of time in Europe, especially Austria, and, like Graves, was elected Professor of Poetry at Oxford University. His many volumes of poetry are all published by Faber; his own selection is published in a Penguin edition.

During the 1930s Auden became known as the most brilliant and original poet of his generation, whose influence on the thinking of intellectuals went far beyond normal readers of poetry. George Macbeth refers to the sheer bulk of his writing, which is 'in the last analysis perhaps the most remarkable thing about him. No other modern English poet has ever tried to do half the things which Auden has done, and he matches Tennyson in the range of his forms and metres from drama and narrative verse to sonnets, songs and prose poems.'

1   **Night Mail** (written to accompany a documentary film)
    (a) Read the poem aloud: how does Auden convey the sensation of the train's movement?
    (b) Discuss the effect of personifying machinery in 'Shovelling white steam over her shoulder', 'blank-faced coaches', 'the steam-tugs yelping', etc.

2   **No Change Of Place**
    (a) Compare the landscape described here with that of *Night Mail*. How would you describe its 'atmosphere'? Which details in particular cause you to form this impression?
    (b) Do the following two poems share this atmosphere?
    (c) Compare *Order To View* and *Débâcle* by Louis Macneice.
    Auden referred to the 1930s as an 'Age of Anxiety', caused by the destruction and pollution brought by industrialization and the threat of war posed by the rise to power of Mussolini and Hitler. Initially, some intellectuals saw Communism as a possible answer to the crisis they saw arising from Man's greed, his pre-occupation with the present, with the materialistic, and the Spanish Civil War became a focal point for their idealism. Later Auden and many of his contemporaries became disillusioned with Communism, their concern being not narrowly political, rather a striving to find peace and content: their message was 'We must love one another or die'—Man must look to love, comradeship, community as his aims, and, like Lawrence, Auden speaks for the power of imagination as a means of achieving them.

3   **Ode/Embassy**
    (a) What contrasts are presented in these poems?
    (b) They were written in the 1930s. Some people think them 'prophetic'. Why?

4   **O What Is That Sound**
    (a) Discuss Auden's use of the ballad form and its effectiveness in telling a story dramatically, paying especial attention to the rhythm and use of repetition. How does the 'story' emerge? (Cf. *The Collier's Wife* by D. H. Lawrence.)

5   **Refugee Blues**
    (a) Which events do you think this poem refers to?
    (b) Why is the 'blues' form more effective here, say, than a ballad metre would have been?

6   **Epitaph On A Tyrant**
    (a) The second line probably refers to Hitler's speeches at the Nuremburg Rallies. Is it important to be aware of this reference when reading the poem?
    (b) Compare *Innocents Song* by Charles Causley.

7   **Surgical Ward/Musée Des Beaux Arts**
    (a) Discuss Auden's views on suffering presented in these poems. Do you agree with them?
    (b) Compare *The Building*, by Philip Larkin and *Surgical Ward: Men* by Robert Graves.

8   **The Unknown Citizen**
    (a) How would you describe the tone of this poem? What effect does the rhyming of the ends of lines have on the poem and your reading of it?

(b) What is the meaning of the last line?

(c) How does the poet regard the unknown citizen—with admiration, pity, contempt . . . ?

(d) What does the poem reveal of Auden's feelings towards our civilization? Is the 'State' like this today? Do you know people who would qualify for this 'monument'?

(e) Compare *Prayer Before Birth* by Louis Macneice.

9   **As I Walked Out One Evening/Our Bias/If I Could Tell You**
(a) What do these poems have in common, and how do they differ?

(b) What is the significance of the references to lions? (Cf. also *Ode*.)

(c) Does Auden share Hardy's attitude towards the passing of time?

(d) Compare also the first group of poems by Louis Macneice below, and *An Arundel Tomb*, by Philip Larkin.

10 **Seascape**
Look carefully at the arrangement of the lines of this poem, and listen closely to the sounds made by the words when spoken, in such phrases as 'The leaping light for your delight', 'The swaying sound of the sea' and in the whole of the second stanza; then discuss how Auden uses his craft to bring his scene vividly to the 'stranger's' imagination, so that we can perceive the sheer drop of the cliff, the particular movements Auden notices in the sea, the gull and the ships. (Cf. *Winter Seascape* by John Betjeman.)

Louis Macneice (1907–64)

Macneice taught Classics at Birmingham and London Universities and worked for 24 years for the BBC as a writer and producer of feature programmes. His work is often spoken of in the same breath as Auden's and he is widely regarded as the most important poet of the 1930s after Auden; he visited Spain in 1936, but was never so deeply committed to left-wing politics as Auden. His poetry is published by Faber, including a Collected edition of his works (1966). His radio play *The Dark Tower* is regarded by many as the best piece of writing ever achieved for radio, and a recording of the original production is occasionally repeated.

1   **Autobiography/Soap Suds/Solstice**
(a) What impressions do you form from reading these poems of Macneice and his feelings concerning time?

(b) How are these feelings expressed in the poems that follow?

(c) Compare the final group of poems in the selection of Auden above, *Rising Early*, by Robert Graves, and the poems by Thomas Hardy.

2   **Snow/The Sunlight On The Garden**
(a) 'The drunkenness of things being various': how are the ideas of this poem echoed in the poetry of Laurie Lee?

(b) What is the significance of the last line of *Snow*?

(c) Is the meaning of this poem the same as that of *Solstice* and *The Sunlight On The Garden*?

(d) Look closely at the rhyme scheme of *The Sunlight On The Garden*: what effect does it have when the poem is read aloud, and how does this effect contribute to the poem's meaning?

('We are dying, Egypt, dying' is a reference to Anthony's last words in Shakespeare's *Anthony and Cleopatra*: after the flight of the Egyptian squadron at Actium and the defeat of his troops by Caesar, he has been falsely told of Cleopatra's death and kills himself.)

3 **Les Sylphides**
(a) How has the poet related his own experience to the ballet? (Compare Hardy's use of landscape in his poetry.)
(b) What is the significance of the opening line, 'Life in a day'?

4 **Order To View/Débâcle**
(a) What atmosphere is created by the images in *Order To View*?
(b) Is this merely a description of an experience, or is the building symbolic—as in *Débâcle*? (Both poems were written in 1940.)
(c) Compare *No Change Of Place* by W. H. Auden, and *The Haunted House* by Robert Graves.

5 **Prayer Before Birth**
(a) Do you think the unborn child's fears are justified?
(b) What are the effects of the internal rhymes (e.g. 'bat'/'rat') and the visual pattern on your reading of the poem?
(c) Compare this poem with *The Unknown Citizen* by W. H. Auden: does a similar view of mankind appear there?
(d) Compare also *Born Yesterday* by Philip Larkin, and *Mary, Mary Magdalene* by Charles Causley.

6 **Cradle Song For Eleanor**
Compare these lines from Auden's *The Witnesses*:

You are the town and We are the clock.
We are the guardians of the gate in the rock,
    The Two.
On your left and on your right,
In the day and in the night,
    We are watching you. . . .
We've been watching you over the garden wall
    For hours:
The sky is darkening like a stain;
Something is going to fall like rain,
    And it won't be flowers.

When the green field comes off like a lid,
Revealing what was much better hid—
    Unpleasant:
And look, behind you without a sound
The woods have come up and are standing round
    In deadly crescent.

The bolt is sliding in its groove;
Outside the window is the black remov-
ers van;
And now with sudden swift emergence
Come the hooded women, the hump-backed surgeons,
    And the Scissor Man.

This might happen any day;
So be careful what you say
    And do:
Be clean, be tidy, oil the lock,
Weed the garden, wind the clock;
    Remember the Two.

7 **After The Crash/Budgie**
(a) 'It was too late to die'. What do you think is meant by this line, and how is it echoed in *Budgie*?
(b) What is the connection between the second poem and *Prayer Before Birth*?

8 **The Gardener**
(a) Discuss your impressions of the gardener and of the poet's attitude towards him.
(b) Compare this poem with *Dick Straightup* by Ted Hughes.

9 **The Wiper**
Discuss the imagery of this poem: is it just a description of a view through a car window? What do you understand

'While we, dazzled by darkness,
Haul the black future toward us
Peeling the skin from our hands;
    And yet we hold the road'

to mean?

John Betjeman (1906–   )

Betjeman is the Poet Laureate and perhaps the best-known and the best-selling English poet of this century (Philip Larkin also regards him as the best English poet now writing). Apart from his reputation as a poet, Betjeman is known as a leading authority on Victorian architecture who has done more than anyone else to revive interest in and prevent the destruction of many beautiful and important buildings of the nineteenth century. His *Collected Poems* (1970), *Summoned By Bells* (1960) and *A Nip In The Air* (1975) are published by John Murray. He has made two LPs for Charisma Records, on which he reads his poems to the accompaniment of the music of Jim Parker.

1 **Pot Pourri From A Surrey Garden/A Subaltern's Love Song/Indoor Games Near Newbury**
(a) Discuss what you find amusing in these poems.
(b) They are set in the English Home Counties in the 1930s. How does the poet feel towards the society he describes and its behaviour? Does he mock or tease the girls—and himself?
(c) What is conveyed by the poems' rhythms? (The third poem is read by the poet to the accompaniment of the music of Jim Parker on *Betjeman's Banana Blush*—Charisma Records CAS 1086.)

176

2 **Winter Seascape/Greenaway**
(a) Compare these two seascapes, paying particular attention to their use of rhyme and rhythm, and the arrangement of the lines.
(b) What makes lines like
   'And thunder under in a cave'
and
   'Before the next can fully burst
   The shooting surf comes hissing round'
particularly effective when read aloud? Could a similar effect be achieved in prose? The poet has said,
> 'My verse is made to be said out loud. I regard verse as the shortest and most memorable way of saying things—or rather that is what I think it ought to be. I also prefer to use rhythm and traditional forms as I think that until you know and can use rhyme and metre, you cannot know from what you are breaking free to write "free verse", nor distinguish between poetry and prose.'

(c) Compare W. H. Auden, *Seascape*.

3 **East Anglian Bathe/Sunday Morning, King's Cambridge**
Discuss how these poems appeal to our senses, helping us to imagine vividly the scenes described (read the poems aloud first).

4 **Bristol and Clifton**
(a) What impressions do you form of the speakers in this poem?
(b) Betjeman lets the churchwarden speak for himself, without making any direct comment: can you nevertheless deduce the poet's attitude towards the subject of his poem?

5 **The Village Inn/Inexpensive Progress**
(a) How does the tone of these poems differ from that of the previous poems in this selection?
(b) What does Betjeman value in buildings, and what does he detest?
(c) Compare *Going, Going* by Philip Larkin.

6 **Death In Leamington/On A Portrait Of A Deaf Man/A Child Ill**
(a) What do these poems add to your impressions of the poet that you have formed from reading the previous poems in this selection?
(b) What does the setting of *Death In Leamington* contribute to the poem's total effect?
   (The 'deaf man' of the second poem was the poet's father.)

Philip Larkin (1922–)

Larkin is librarian at Hull University. He is generally considered as the central figure of the group known as The Movement, who began publishing widely in the mid-1950s, and whose verse aimed at achieving a cool elegance of form and diction expressing a lucid intelligence and avoiding what they considered to be the excessive displays of emotion shown in much of the poetry written in the 1940s. Larkin's volumes of poetry are *The Less Deceived* (Marvell Press, 1955), *The Whitsun Weddings* (Faber, 1964), *The North Ship* (Faber, 1966) and *High Windows* (Faber, 1974).

1 **Born Yesterday/Days**
(a) Compare the hopes of *Born Yesterday* with the fears of Louis Macneice's *Prayer Before Birth*.
(b) What is your definition of 'happiness'—and how can it be achieved?
(c) What do you think is meant by the last stanza of *Days*, especially the effect of the words 'long coats' as they are used here?
(d) How is *Days* similar to the poetry of R. S. Thomas?

2 **To The Sea/The Whitsun Weddings**
(a) Discuss the poet's attitude towards the families he describes in these poems. What feelings are aroused in him by what he sees?
(b) He is an admirer of the poetry of John Betjeman: is there any similarity between the poets evident here?
(c) How do you interpret the final image of *The Whitsun Weddings*?

3 **Mr Bleaney**
(a) What impressions do you form of Mr Bleaney, and of the narrator?
(b) What connection is there between this poem and the closing lines of *Afternoons*?

4 **Afternoons/Skin/An Arundel Tomb**
(a) Discuss Larkin's attitude to the passing of time as expressed in these poems (cf. the poems of Hardy, Graves, Auden and Macneice cited above).
(b) How has 'Time transfigured' the earl and countess into 'untruth' in *An Arundel Tomb*? What are the effects of time that Larkin notices here, and how does the poem create the sensation of time passing? What do the poem's rhyme scheme and rhythm contribute to its total effect?

5 **The Building**
(a) Why is the purpose of the building not made clear in the title of the poem?
(b) What is the attitude of the people who use the building? Larkin refers to the 'unseen congregations': is there any similarity between the 'endless altered people' of the previous poem and the people who use this building?
(c) What is meant by

> 'unless its powers
> Outbuild cathedrals nothing contravenes
> The coming dark'?

and what is the tone of

> 'O world,
> Your loves, your chances, are beyond the stretch
> Of any hand from here'?

(read the preceding sentence first: what effect does it have on the lines quoted here?) What is meant by the sentence that follows?
(d) Which features of the building and its atmosphere does the poet emphasize?

(e) What is his attitude towards the people who enter it?
(f) Does a similar attitude emerge towards the people described in *To The Sea/The Whitsun Weddings* and *Mr Bleaney*?

6   **Going, Going**
(a) Compare this poem with *Progress*, by John Betjeman.
(b) Do you share the poets' feelings as you look at the country in which you live?

7   **The Trees/The Explosion**
(a) How is what the trees 'seem to say' similar to the wives' vision after the explosion?
(b) What do the poems mean to you as you compare them with what Larkin says in the other poems in this selection? Do you see them as an expression of hope?

R. S. Thomas (1913–   )

R. S. Thomas has lived his life as an Anglican priest, often working in isolated agricultural parishes whose 'tough, hard, narrow men' appear in his poetry. A newspaper interview referred to his being saddened by the gradual disappearance of their way of life and seeing the Industrial Revolution as the beginning of the end for Wales—'One knows it is all rather hopeless, but one feels it all the same. Reason may say that science and progress are valuable—they relieve hunger, and so on—yet one's feelings, the poetry in one, seem to say something quite different, beyond reason.' Rupert Hart-Davis published the following volumes of his verse: *Song At The Year's Turning* (1956), *Poetry For Supper* (1958), *Tare* (1961), *The Bread Of Truth* (1963), *Pietà* (1966), *Not That He Brought Flowers* (1969), and Macmillan *H'm* (1972). A selection of his poetry is included in *Penguin Modern Poets 1*.

1   **Song/Soil**
(a) How do these poems contrast one another, and how are the thoughts of the first poem echoed by other poets represented in this anthology?
(b) Are the people described in the poems that follow to be included in the 'men' referred to here? A critic in a newspaper article wrote:
> 'The characteristic conflict of R. S. Thomas's poetry is between the instinctual life of the Welsh peasant, rooted deep in the earth, and the menaces of civilization. . . . R. S. Thomas clings to an ideal of simple living.'
Discuss how this ideal is expressed in the following poems. What does the poet value in 'the instinctual life of the Welsh peasant', and how is it menaced?
(c) Compare his view of the countryside with Laurie Lee's. In another poem, Thomas writes about sheep:

> Yes, I know. They are like primroses;
> Their ears are the colour of the stems
> Of primroses; and their eyes—
> Two halves of a nut.
>   But images
> Like this are for sheer fancy
> To play with. Seeing how Wales fares

Now, I will attend rather
To things as they are: to green grass
That is not ours; to visitors
Buying us up. . . .
                    What would they say
Who bled here, warriors
Of a free people?

Relate these lines to the poems included in this selection: what does Laurie Lee 'attend to' in his verse?

2   **Welsh Landscape/Depopulation Of The Hills/The Village/Affinity**
    (a) Discuss the picture of Wales and the poet's feelings towards his country that emerge in these poems. How does the landscape compare with that of Hardy's and Larkin's verse?
    (b) What is the 'world' referred to in the last stanza of *The Village* and the 'affinity' in the last poem of this group? What is 'the old hunger, born of his kind'?

3   **The Last Of The Peasantry/The Poacher/The Lonely Farmer/A Peasant/Invasion On The Farm**
    (a) Discuss how these portraits of individuals develop the ideas of *Affinity* and the other poems grouped above.
    (b) Compare the people's similarities and differences. (Iago Prytherch seems to be a composite figure, a character appearing in several of Thomas's poems.)
    (c) Compare *The Lonely Farmer* with Hardy's *The Darkling Thrush*: do both poets make similar comparisons with the bird?
    (d) Is Thomas's attitude towards the people he describes similar to that of Philip Larkin in his poems?

4   **Cynddylan On A Tractor**
    (a) Do you think the poet admires Cynddylan?
    (b) In a poem addressed to Iago Prytherch, he asks:

                        'Can't you see
    Behind the smile on the times' face
    The cold brain of the machine
    That will destroy you and your race?'

    Is the same question relevant here?

5   **Death Of A Peasant/The Evacuee**
    The poet is also a priest, working in Wales. What do these poems (and the preceding ones) tell you about the community in which he works and his feelings towards his people?

Laurie Lee (1918–   )

Laurie Lee was the youngest but one of a family of eight, and was educated at the village school in Slad, Gloucestershire and at Stroud Central School, which he left at fifteen to run a local dance band, before leaving home to seek his fortune: the

walk to London took him a month. After working as a builder's labourer, he went
to Spain (he was there when the Civil War broke out) and returned there a year
later by walking across the Pyrenees. These experiences (and many more) form the
basis of his best-selling *Cider With Rosie* and *As I Walked Out*. A selection of his
poetry is published by Studio Vista. Many of the poems included here are read
aloud by the poet on an Argo recording of a poetry and jazz concert.

1 **Thistles**
Compare this poem with Ted Hughes' on the same subject.

2 **First Love/Milkmaid/April Rise/Day Of These Days/Apples**
(a) Read the poems aloud: how does the poet appeal to our senses in
imagining the details of the landscape he describes?
(b) What do these poems celebrate in nature? How does their viewpoint
compare with those of other poets included in this anthology—for instance,
Hughes and Lawrence?

3 **Cock Pheasant/Town Owl**
(a) Compare Laurie Lee's reactions to these two birds. Why are they compared
with 'an Inca priest' and 'an augur'?
(b) Does Ted Hughes notice similar qualities in the animals he writes about?

4 **Sunken Evening**
Discuss how the poem develops the image introduced in its title.

5 **Field Of Autumn/Christmas Landscape**
(a) Compare these poems with those about spring and summer (in 2 above).
Discuss what is emphasized in these descriptions, and the poet's choice of
details in his landscape and use of sound to convey his impressions.

6 **The Long War**
(a) Discuss what this poem says about war and its effect on people.
(b) Do other poems in this volume have a similar message?

Charles Causley (1917–   )

Causley wrote his first poems while in the Royal Navy, and much of his poetry
looks back to his experiences as a seaman in the Second World War. He is
Headteacher of a primary school in his native Cornwall. His earlier volumes of
poetry, *Union Street* (1957) and *Johnny Allelulia* (1961) were published by Hart-
Davis: *Underneath The Water* (1967), *Figure Of Eight* (1969), *Figgie Hobbin* (1973)
and his 'Collected Poems 1951–1975' by Macmillan. A selection of his poetry is
included in *Penguin Modern Poets 3*.

1 **The Seasons In North Cornwall/Mary, Mary Magdalene**
(a) Notice the characteristics of Causley's landscape that appear in his poetry
and compare his 'use' of these features with other poets in this anthology (e.g.
Hardy and Betjeman).
(b) What is suggested to you by the imagery of these poems?

2 **By St Thomas Water/Reservoir Street** ('cloam' = the clay used for making an earthenware oven (for baking bread, etc.) built into the side of an old-fashioned open hearth)/**Dockacre**
(a) '. . . the same malaise that even death won't cure'. Tell one another of experiences or events you have read about that you are reminded of when reading these poems.
(b) How does the 'malaise' recur in other poems in this selection?

3 **Nursery Rhyme Of Innocence And Experience**
Compare Causley's use of the ballad form here with other poems in this selection (cf. also Auden's *O What Is That Sound*). What are the special characteristics of this verse form?

4 **John Polruddon/Innocent's Song/Charlotte Dymond/Cowboy Song**
(a) Is the 'smiling stranger' present (perhaps implicitly) in other poems in this selection?
(b) What are the similarities in the experiences described in these poems?
(John Polruddon's house was on the cliff over Pentewan, in south Cornwall. The story of his disappearance dates from early Tudor times)

5 **Death Of A Poet** (Louis Macneice)/**Song Of The Dying Gunner** ('Aggie Weston's' = hostels for sailors established in naval ports by Dame Agnes Weston; 'Guz' = Devonport; 'A.A.1' = Anti-Aircraft Gunner, 1st Class; 'tiddly suit' = sailor's best shore-going uniform with gold badges.)/**Convoy/Death Of An Aircraft**
(a) What do these poems tell us of Causley's attitude to death, and war? (Compare them with those of Wilfred Owen, Robert Graves, W. H. Auden and Ted Hughes)
(b) Discuss your reactions to these images:
'Over the church a bell broke like a wave upended.
The hearse left for winter with a lingering hiss'   (*Death Of A Poet*)
'And the three ships
Come sailing in'   (*Convoy*)
'Scrubbed his face with perpetual dark
And rubbed it out like a pencil mark'   (*Death Of An Aircraft*)
(c) Discuss other images in Causley's poems that you find particularly vivid and forceful.
(d) 'In prime condition
To take on a load of ammunition'

'A glass of wine for the afternoon
With permission to sing a signature tune'

'The soldier's silver shilling earned
And, armed like an archangel, returned'

Locate these lines from *Death Of An Aircraft* in their contexts, then discuss your understanding of their meanings, paying particular attention to the phrases 'in prime condition', 'a signature tune' and 'armed like an archangel'. What do you find to be ironical in this poem?

Ted Hughes (1930–   )

Hughes, born in Yorkshire, has said that 'what excites my imagination is the war between vitality and death'; the critic A. E. Dyson refers to the poet's dual concerns of power and violence—'He is fascinated by violence of all kinds, in love and in hatred, in the jungle and the arena in battle, murder and sudden death. Violence, for him, is the occasion not for reflection, but for being; it is a guarantee of energy, of life, and most so, paradoxically, when it knows itself in moments of captivity, pain or death.' The American poet, Robert Lowell, has said that Hughes's animal poems are 'like a thunderbolt', appearing to spring from the page with the energy of a force of nature, and Edward Lucie-Smith refers to his 'characteristic gift for writing about the natural world from the inside, as a being who knows that he is not divided from it. Hughes's work achieves its force through the way in which one image detonates another, so that the whole poem throbs with controlled violence.' He is generally regarded, with Philip Larkin, as one of the two most important English poets to have appeared since the Second World War. All his poetry is published by Faber (including a selection in paperback): *Hawk In The Rain* (1957), *Lupercal* (1960), *Wodwo* (1967), *Crow* (1970).

1   **The Thought-Fox**
    (a) What is the subject of this poem?
    (b) Notice how Hughes arranges the order of his words and lines to enact the movement of the fox. Can you find further examples in his poems about animals?
    (c) Compare *Snake* and *Bat* by D. H. Lawrence.

2   **Wind/November/Crow Hill**
    (a) What are the distinctive features of the landscape of these poems and the language used to describe it? Notice especially the verbs used to describe the wind and rain and the characteristic sound texture of the words when spoken aloud, as in

> 'Buttoned from the blowing mist
> Walk the ridges of ruined stone'.

    (b) What fascinates the poet about the tramp?

3   **Hawk Roosting/Thrushes/Esther's Tomcat/Pike**
    (a) What do the creatures described in these poems have in common?
    (b) How are these lines from *Jaguar* reflected in this group of poems?

> 'He spins from bars, but there's no cage to him
> More than to the visionary his cell:
> His stride is wildernesses of freedom:
> The world rolls under the long thrust of his heel.
> Over the cage floor the horizons come.'

    (c) 'No arguments assert my right': compare *Her Husband*. How do these creatures compare with humans?
    (d) Discuss what Hughes admires in these creatures: do the poems show only admiration, or are other emotions present as well?
    (c) Compare Lawrence's animal poems, especially *Snake* and *Kangaroo*.

4   **Snowdrop/Her Husband/Thistles**
   (a) What is similar in the nature of the conflicts described in these poems, and in the images and wounds of the words used to describe them? (Cf. *Pike*.)
   (b) Compare *Thistles* with Laurie Lee's poem on the same subject, and *Christmas Landscape*.

5   **Bayonet Charge/Six Young Men**
   (a) Compare *Bayonet Charge* with the descriptions of war by Wilfred Owen.
   (b) Discuss what you understand to be the meaning of the last stanza of *Six Young Men*. How is this idea echoed in the poetry of Charles Causley?
   (c) Compare also *Recalling War* by Robert Graves.

6   **Dick Straightup/The Bull Moses**
   (a) Discuss what the poet admires in the person described in the first poem and the connection between this figure and the subject of the following poem. (Compare the figures that people the poetry of R. S. Thomas also.)
   (b) 'Blackness is depth beyond star': is this the same darkness that appears in *Pike*? (Compare also *Bavarian Gentians* by D. H. Lawrence.)

7   **The Horses**
   (a) Read this poem aloud: how does the poet use sounds to emphasize the distinctive quality of the sight he describes? How do the arrangement of the lines and the imagery reinforce this quality?
   (b) Why do you think the poet wants to remember this experience
      'In din of crowded streets, going among the years, the faces'?